God the Source of Good

A Guide to Trusting that from God all Good Flows

Henry Thomas Hamblin

Hamblin Vision Publishing

Copyright

© Copyright 2025 Hamblin Vision Publishing - all rights reserved.

The content contained within this book may not be reproduced, duplicated or transmitted without direct written permission from the author or the publisher.

Under no circumstances will any blame or legal responsibility be held against the publisher, or author, for any damages, reparation, or monetary loss due to the information contained within this book, either directly or indirectly.

Legal Notice:

This book is copyright protected. It is only for personal use. You cannot amend, distribute, sell, use, quote or paraphrase any part, or the content within this book, without the consent of the author or publisher.

Disclaimer Notice:

Please note the information contained within this document is for educational and entertainment purposes only. All effort has been executed to present accurate, up to date, reliable, complete information. No warranties of any kind are declared or implied. Readers acknowledge that the author is not engaged in the rendering of legal, financial, medical or professional advice. The content within this book has been derived from various sources. Please consult a licensed professional before attempting any techniques outlined in this book.

By reading this document, the reader agrees that under no circumstances is the author responsible for any losses, direct or indirect, that are incurred as a result of the use of the information contained within this document, including, but not limited to, errors, omissions, or inaccuracies.

Contents

Introduction	VII
Concise Biography of Henry Thomas Hamblin	IX

Part 1: God's Sustaining Grace

1.	God, our Source	2
2.	God's Presence	5
3.	God, the Unchanging	11
4.	God, the Power Within Us	14
5.	God, the Liberator	17
6.	God, the Unfailing	20
7.	God, our Help and Inward Power	22
8.	God, the Good	25
9.	God, the Rewarder	27
10.	God, our Father-Mother	32

Part 2: God, our Centre and Source

11.	One Central Source	36
12.	God, the Giver of Life	39

13. God, as Love	41
14. God, our Source of Victory	44
15. God, our Source of Protection	46
16. God, our Source of Stability	49
17. God, our Source of Substance	51
18. God, our Rock	57
19. God, our Source of Health	65
20. God, our Source of Abundance	68
Part 3: God the Infinite Good	
21. The Infinite Good	78
22. Our Highest Good	90
23. Divine Good	100
Also by Henry Thomas Hamblin	111

Introduction

By Noel Raine, Chair of the Hamblin Trust

H.T. Hamblin was a prolific author of a range of books, booklets, and pamphlets offering practical advice on how to live in harmony with God, or what he sometimes referred to as Source, the Universe, or the Cosmic. However, this was not just a spiritual quest, or an attempt to avoid the troubles and cares of everyday life – far from it, for Hamblin was a very practical mystic – but a practical guide for each one to follow to increase health, happiness, and prosperity.

Hamblin founded the Science of Thought Institute, offering a course of practical lessons intended to guide his many thousands of students towards a happier, healthier, and more prosperous life. Although he is sadly no longer with us in person, he left a wonderful legacy of publications that he had written from 1921 up to the time of his death in 1958. Some of those are still in print and available from The Hamblin Trust at www.thehamblinvision.org.uk, but many have since gone out of print.

Conscious that the Trust will not be around forever, the custodians of Hamblin's teachings — the trustees of the Hamblin Trust — have decided to produce copies of Hamblin's earlier works in digital format to leave a legacy for future generations. Whilst the style of writing may now seem a little dated, Hamblin's teachings remain valid and, although edited a little to bring them more into line with current editorial style, we are pleased to bring you, in one compilation, three of Hamblin's earlier booklets offering a guide to a deeper, happier, and joy-filled life:

- *God Our Centre and Source* (First published in 1943)

- *God the Infinite Good* (First published in 1944)

- *God's Sustaining Grace* (First published in 1933)

The three small books in this compilation offer Hamblin's personal insights on how they can be used to transform our lives, both spiritually and practically, leading to greater health, happiness, and joy. It is our hope that this compilation will, indeed, help you to achieve the health and happiness that the application of Hamblin's teachings can provide, and the sheer joy that arises from living in accordance with the simple spiritual insights he shares.

Many blessings for health, harmony, and joy.

Noel Raine
Chair of the Trustees
The Hamblin Trust

Concise Biography of Henry Thomas Hamblin

By John Delafield, Hamblin's Grandson

Who was Henry Thomas Hamblin?

Henry Thomas Hamblin was a spiritual teacher and writer based in Sussex, England, whose message and vision were straightforward and pragmatic. He believed that the spiritual life and the practical, everyday life were inseparable. His teachings centred around the power of thought and the importance of meditation to draw on the inner power, wisdom and love that we all have deep within us. Hamblin referred to this as 'the Secret Place of the Most High' in the days before meditation was widely practised in the West.

Hamblin was colloquially known as HTH, and later 'the Saint of Sussex'. Whilst his teachings leaned towards esoteric Christianity, his philosophy was truly universal, embracing the truths of all faiths. The emphasis of his message is on finding the power of spirituality within us all, in the context of our everyday lives, rather than religion. As a young man, he reacted against the dogma of his strict, religious upbringing, and believed that religion often divided people, while spirituality united people. His teachings came from a place of pure empathy and compassion for humankind.

Henry Thomas Hamblin worked right up to the end of his life in 1958 and left a legacy that continues to this day, its voice as much needed now as it ever was.

A Wayward Child

Henry Thomas Hamblin was born in 1873 in Walworth, South East London, of Kentish parents, and was the second of two sons. His father was very religious, and his grandfather a minister of the Baptist Church. His mother, although of diminutive size, was reportedly 'great of soul' and ruled the family with benevolent autocracy. The family was poor, very poor, like all those living around them in that district of London in the late Victorian era, and, despite their hard work, the only education that could be afforded for Henry was an elementary one. He followed this with a course in technology, which proved to be of inestimable value to a youth who was considered by his parents and teachers to be wayward.

"Unstable as water; thou shall not excel," his mother reproached him regularly. No doubt she intended it to shame her son into a regime of self-improvement, in keeping with child-rearing practices of the time, but it was hardly confidence-inspiring! "Slacker!" was the repeated insult from his elder brother. Wiser, more objective, heads might have paused for long enough to recognise a certain potential in the young boy who, at the age of nine, could attempt the writing of a school newspaper. He had also established himself as something of an elocutionist. Writing and speaking would both prove valuable skills in later life.

His adolescent years gave little indication of an error in the family verdict. 'Henry the wayward' moved from one poorly-paid post to another, idled in between dead-end jobs, succumbed to bouts of ill-health, and, before he had reached the age of eighteen, had displayed more than the usual 'adolescent failings', according to his autobiography, *The Story of My Life*. From a modern perspective, all these Victorian euphemisms point to Hamblin being something of a 'bad lad', an impression added to by his own heavy hints that he had been no stranger to drinking and carousing. He suffered terribly from pangs of regret following his periods of over-indulgence, so that 'Henry the sinner' became 'Henry the saint' – until the next time. His pronounced rebellious streak landed him in hot water more than once. He constantly pushed against the boundaries of the fire-and-brimstone brand of Christianity in which he had been raised, which he felt to be unbearably restrictive. Reading about his struggles with authority as a young man somehow makes the rather aloof spiritual writer he became more accessible and endearing; it's hard not to warm to someone who so openly confesses their own faults and shortcomings, especially in the tightly buttoned-up era in which he lived. He was inspired by books, many of which fired his worldly ambition and prompted his spiritual imagination.

What his parents and educators overlooked was that Hamblin was a young man with huge aspiration, flushed with a youthful zest for life, and inspired by a worthy ambition to rise above the rut of his circumstances. Although he pushed against his father's dogmatic and punitive style of practising religion, at heart, he was deeply religious. A person's early environment, education, and adolescent behaviour can often determine the course of their life. Youthful indulgences of one sort or another are inevitable. Hamblin's studies of the New Testament, which revealed that selfishness and hypocrisy, rather than indulgence, received greater condemnation by Jesus, would have been very much in his consciousness.

A Successful Businessman

There is no doubt that Hamblin had an enquiring mind, and this, coupled with a desire for scientific accuracy, enabled him to achieve success in his later endeavours in business. In this, despite his lack of education, he was bolstered by boundless faith and courage, which, coupled with a shrewd business sense, ensured that he succeeded beyond all expectation. In 1898, having taught himself ophthalmics at night, he qualified as an optician and set up his first successful business as an optician, Theodore Hamblin (now Dolland and Aitchison), frequented by royalty, the rich and the famous.

Hamblin was a natural entrepreneur and a born risk-taker. By this time, he was also a family man. He married Eva Elizabeth in 1902, and they went on to have two sons and a daughter. He enjoyed acquiring several businesses, all with insufficient capital, and relying on credit and goodwill. He took more pleasure in the thrill of the challenge than in the promise of monetary gain. Far from being downcast in the face of numerous setbacks, he thrived on negotiating obstacles which appeared insurmountable. As soon as the business was established and running smoothly, however, rather than being satisfied with financial security and the ability to provide for his family, Hamblin's interest started to wane. He felt a loss of the initial drive and motivation, his physical and mental health began to decline... until the next big idea came along and away he would charge again, all fired up and raring to go.

Throughout all his wild days of youth and high-risk business ventures, Hamblin felt a great tug towards discovering a deeper meaning to life, beyond that of the daily struggle to make ends meet. Propelled by his discontent, he became a driven seeker after truth. In his quest, he met other prominent thinkers of the time and formed lasting friendships.

As his business success grew, so did a gnawing sense of depression. It was as if there was something inside him that had not yet found a voice. Around this time, he discovered the New Thought movement and began to read their publications. Hamblin realised then that none of his worldly success had made him happy. He felt that a move from London to the coast would be beneficial.

Shortly afterwards came the outbreak of the First World War, and Hamblin went off to serve his country, leaving his business in the care of others, almost with a sense of gleeful relief, strange though it sounds. But it was the sudden and unexpected death of his younger son at the age of ten, in 1918, that brought him to rock bottom and he began to question everything.

A Very Practical Mystic

Hamblin was not a genius, and millions of other people have made good in the world with even less promising assets. But it was in the second half of his life, when Hamblin turned away from creating highly successful business enterprises to focus instead on the spiritual realm, that his unique combination of the pragmatic and the profoundly spiritual shone forth. He has sometimes been described as a very practical mystic.

Hamblin began writing in the 1920s. The words seemed to flow from him. He found that writing clarified his thoughts. One of his first books written in this new phase of his career was *Within You Is The Power*, which was to sell over 200,000 copies. Other books soon followed. Hamblin believed that there is a source of abundance which, when contacted, could change a person's entire life. As long as people blamed their external circumstances for any misfortune, they were stuck in the 'victim role'; but if they moved in harmony with their inner source, their life could be full of abundance and harmony.

Soon after this, Hamblin set up a magazine called *The Science of Thought Review,* based on the principles of Applied Right Thinking. He wasn't discouraged by the fact that he had no experience of editing or publishing. His experience had taught him that if the mind worked in harmony with the Divine, then everything you needed flowed towards you. Anyone with any business sense at all knew that to set up a magazine with a first print run of 10,000 copies would be a risky thing to do. But Hamblin was not risk averse, to put it mildly! He wanted to put what he believed into practice. The only magazine of its kind in the 1920s, it soon gained a worldwide readership. Among his friends and contemporaries that were to contribute to the magazine were Joel Goldsmith, Henry Victor Morgan, Graham Ikin, Clare Cameron and Derek Neville, all of them prolific and successful writers. Apart from his international subscribers, Hamblin had close ties to comparative spiritual thinkers in many other countries, especially in the U.S.

Although he had been brought up in a strictly religious family, he hadn't found any of the answers he sought in the Church. He realised that, rather than following any creed or dogma, which didn't work for him anyway, he had to look within himself. He found contact with 'Presence' and realised it held the key to the peace he was seeking. All the time, his search was leading him nearer to discovering the way his thoughts affected his performance and outlook.

During the General Strike of 1926, the Great Depression of 1929-32, and again in years after the end of the Second World

War, many homeless, unemployed wayfarers came to the Hamblin household seeking relief and shelter. Henry and Elizabeth provided them with a simple meal, new boots and clothing, and money for the road. Hamblin was a man who applied his spiritual principles to his everyday life. Practical Mysticism was Hamblin's life's work. He helped people, in practical ways, to become less fearful, happier, and more successful in their lives. To this end, he wrote books like *The Antidote to Worry*. However, later in life he realised that whilst these books genuinely helped people, they were largely concerned with the personality. He then wished to go a step further and become more fully a truly 'practical mystic', so he wrote a spiritual course of 26 lessons, each with a definite theme presented in a systematic way. This was designed to move beyond the constraints of personality so that the soul could breathe the pure air of Spirit. What was needed, he felt, was 'a total surrender of ourselves to the Divine.' The course is available as the book *The Way of the Practical Mystic*.

The Power of Thought

Hamblin was at the forefront of the New Thought movement which was gaining pace in the early 20th century. He discovered that 'new thought' was, in fact, ancient wisdom, based upon the truth that has always existed since before time began. All great souls give voice to that timeless truth in a myriad of different ways. Hamblin urges us to "Think in harmony with the Universal

Mind." In other words, he underlines the fact that truth is and cannot be changed depending upon our mood or our whim.

Hamblin realised that we need not only a positive frame of mind but an applied way of thinking - Right Thinking, as he termed it. What did he mean by that? Essentially, he defines Right Thinking as:

- Thinking from the Divine standpoint.

- Controlling the thoughts so they do not go off on negative tangents away from the Divine Truth, which is always positive.

- Replacing negative thoughts with positive thoughts.

- Living in the consciousness that all is well; and as an adjunct to this, remembering that perfection exists as a reality now, and to think in the consciousness of that knowledge.

- Meditation or prayer is the highest form of Right Thinking.

- Ultimately, however, the aim is to get beyond thought, 'to enter ultimate truth'.

He said, "When we cease thinking, we glide out on the ocean of God's Peace. Thought brings us to the foot of the mountain after which we have to proceed by intuition."

Health, Wealth and Happiness. Isn't this something we all want, either for ourselves or for those dear to us? And yet, how many of us are struggling to reach or hold such a goal for a sustained period of time?'

Hamblin's teachings explain how we can achieve all of these things, not by hard work and striving but by a simple change of thought. *Within You is the Power* is one of his simple but profound statements, and the title of one of his books.

Hamblin was a prolific author and had many thousands of followers studying and benefiting from his teachings and courses until his death in 1958. The simple principles contained in those teachings are as relevant today as they were when he was alive, and can still help us to achieve health, prosperity and happiness if we apply them conscientiously.

He died in 1958 in Chichester Hospital. The Hamblin Trust exists to this day to propagate the legacy of his work.

The Relevance of his Teachings Today

Hamblin was, essentially, a Christian mystic, yet his ideas about the simplicity and clarity of presence seem incredibly contemporary. He believed that the source of all wisdom is within us and all around us, and that this is the fundamental reality; there is no separation, and we are all one. His message and advice to all who read his work is that it is for everyone and is in harmony with the aspiration of all good people throughout time. Hamblin believed that there can be no finite creed of an infinite faith. Moreover, he suggests that, when creeds appear, true faith can be constrained.

He cautioned that if you seek God in prayer, the corollary is that you must have faith in Him. He often stressed that no prayer goes unanswered, and, although you may not get the answer requested, your prayer will be answered in some form. God is around us and within us, and this is the fundamental reality. He made it clear that, although human organisations come and go, God's laws are eternal, and that God is the quintessence of love, wisdom, and harmony. He expresses the clear view that "Blessed are they who believe and yet have not seen". The knowledge that God is born within us is fundamental to our understanding, and only by the loss of self can God be found. At the point a person surrenders his or her 'self' to God, it is then that a re-birth takes place and one's real life in God begins.

Some may question this view and ask: "What is this but the core teachings of the many brands of Christianity?" In response, Hamblin's view was that modern Christianity is a heterogeneous compound of the teachings of Jesus interwoven with historic pagan-based doubts and fears, litanies, supplications and more, all of which are closely guarded by a priestly hierarchy. These were strong views, and Hamblin does not disparage those who found them uncomfortable, as he says that churches are necessary and helpful for those who are succoured by them. Hamblin had a lifelong rebellious streak where authority was concerned, and this included the strictures of the Church. Hamblin would sometimes say that the Truth of the message of Jesus was so often wrapped up in dogma and creed that its purity and simplicity were obscured.

In his teaching, he states that first comes purity of intention, reminding his readers that one cannot serve God and Mammon. Either you trust God completely or you hedge your bets by having worldly alliances and a healthy bank balance. He maintains that trying to achieve both will impair spiritual development. Secondly, an individual's dedication to following God's path will require great patience, perseverance, faith and courage; but in following this path, the individual will develop forbearance and good will. He adds that other life experiences will follow naturally and lead to a developing compassion, which will enable the individual to radiate the love of God.

Where should we place Hamblin in the long line of mystics, seekers and finders? Perhaps it is rather impertinent to pose the question some 65 years after his death, but it is surely relevant to consider this point as, by any measure, he was an extraordinary person.

Remember that he was born into a life of poverty and obscurity but, despite a very limited education, by superhuman efforts of his imagination, he rose to wealth and secured an esteemed position in life, while all the time being aware of another "self" within him, a spiritual self. Dramatically, in the middle part of his life, he surrendered his material successes to follow his wider calling as a disciple of God. In this later life, he did not subscribe to any specific creed or form of religion. He was no haloed saint in the traditional sense, but he would have said, "What I have done, or rather what has been done through me, can be done by any person in the world according to their gifts and personal faith".

The essence of this teaching is that the latent power of God lies within everyone.

John Delafield is the grandson of Henry Thomas Hamblin and a retired RAF pilot. The majority of his childhood was spent living with his grandparents, Henry Thomas and Elizabeth Eva Hamblin.

Part 1: God's Sustaining Grace

Hamblin Vision Publishing

Chapter One

God, our Source

Thy love enfolds me, Thy power upholds me, and Thy wisdom guides me.

Just as there is only one life and source of life, so also is there only one source of supply, and in each case this one source is God.

When we put our whole trust in God for temporal supply, instead of putting our faith in material means, we cease to be at the mercy of the things which are soon exhausted and which pass away, but instead, we are established in that which is eternal and inexhaustible.

One of the greatest illusions of life is that of lack of temporal supply. No child of God can possibly lack any good thing. One who realises this truth, finds that he really can never lack any good thing. He is therefore delivered from the great curse of worry and care over the ways and means of his daily life; and this in turn prevents him from suffering from the diseases which worry and care predispose one to.

In order, however, to realise this truth, and to enjoy a state of freedom from care, it is necessary always to look to God instead of to man.

The one who trusts in the Lord, who is the spiritual creative source of all things and the perpetual fountain of life which sustains all things, both visible and invisible, is blessed, so our text tells us. He is blessed because he puts his trust in that which can never fail, never become exhausted, and which is eternal. He puts his trust in that which is perpetual, unfailing, unalterable wholeness. All our needs are fully and abundantly supplied, both now and always. If we look only to God and realise this truth, we enter into freedom.

> *Blessed is the man that trusts in the Lord, and whose hope the Lord is.*
>
> Jeremiah 17:7

Your presence, O Lord of Light and love and power divine, is always with me, and your spirit goes before me, preparing my way. Because You are nearer than breathing, I am able to commune with You at all times and at any moment. Because You are my Lord and my God, I do all things as an act of worship and as an act of service to the whole. All that I do is done for You and for humanity. My only desire is that I might serve in all faithfulness. Even the smallest tasks and the most irksome duties I perform willingly, for Your sake.

Everything that I do, I do better, because it is done for You. All that I do, I do in love, which is a response to Your greater love for me.

For everything that is necessary for my life I look to the only source of good, and all that I need comes from You. If I need guidance, your wisdom directs me. If I need strength, Your power upholds me. If I need help in difficulty, in the realisation of Your presence, all troubles flee away, and all problems become solved.

Because Your presence is with me, and because I am always abiding in Your presence, no harm can come near me. Evil cannot penetrate Your presence. When Your presence is consciously realised, no evil can find any foothold. I am enfolded in everlasting love, while underneath me are the arms which can never fail.

Chapter Two

God's Presence

When all human and material resources fail, still God remains.

There come times to most of us when all that we usually depend upon fails, and we can only fall back upon God. We may find ourselves in great danger, when all precautions and defences fail and nothing but a miraculous escape can save us. Then, because God is the only one who can deliver us, we put our *whole* trust in Him, and we are delivered. Again, we may be faced by difficulties and problems so great that it is humanly impossible for us to find a way of escape. Then, because to human wisdom, there *is* no way of escape, we trust God so completely and unreservedly that the impossible again becomes divinely possible, and our difficulties are either dissolved away or riven asunder.

Yet again, we may have been so thoroughly beaten and discomforted by "the sin that doth so easily beset us" that there seems no possibility of victory and overcoming. But again, in our extremity, driven by failure and humiliation back upon God, we can only trust Him, for nothing else remains. Then, because of our whole-hearted trust in, and entire dependence upon, God, we are set entirely free, which is indeed the miracle of miracles.

If we would only trust God more and make greater and more daring ventures in faith, then it would not be necessary for us to be driven by life's experiences to the end of our tether. He who goes forward willingly to fresh experiences is not compelled by life's adversities to seek God, for he finds Him of his own volition, and to the joy and satisfaction of his soul.

But, however we go about it, and no matter what our experiences may be, God remains, and is always with us, awaiting our recognition of Him, as a presence of wholeness, of order, of harmony, of peace and joy.

God's Inexhaustibleness

> *They shall not be ashamed in the evil time, and in the days of famine, they shall be satisfied.*
>
> Psalm 37:19.

The psalmist is speaking of the upright, those who think, act and live according to the divine order, generally termed 'righteousness'. He is not referring to the self-righteous who think that they earn and create their own good, but to those who walk with God and acknowledge that all good comes from Him.

There is only one source of good and this is God. God, the one Source, can never be exhausted, He can never fail, for owing to his infinite nature, He is equal to every demand that can be made on Him.

The branch that abides in the vine draws adequate nourishment from the parent stem and is as fruitful as the vine itself. So long as the branch abides in the vine, the difference between them is not one of kind but of degree. But if the branch is severed from the vine, then it soon becomes dried up and useless, except for burning.

It is the same with man. If he is established in the divine, and walks and talks with the Lord, then he is sustained and maintained in the same way that God is, and by the same power and inexhaustibleness. But as soon as he thinks that it is his own self-sufficiency that is upholding him, he becomes separate from his divine source, and rapidly withers away.

Therefore, we have to abide in Him, and thus be constantly connected with the one source of life and power. Then, in the evil day, we are not ashamed, and in the days of famine we are abundantly satisfied.

We can constantly declare that man as a child of God is forever, under grace, in a state of unity and oneness with the one central power and life of the universe, that he draws his life and nourishment entirely from the Lord, and that this omnipotent Source can never fail. Then, "they shall not be ashamed in the evil time (the time of the testing and trying of souls): and in the day of famine (when all material sources fail) they shall be satisfied".

God, the Only Deliverer

> *And it shall come to pass, that whosoever shall call on the name of the Lord shall be delivered.*
>
> Joel 2:32

There is only one deliverer - God, and God alone. So long as we depend, in the slightest degree, upon 'the arm of flesh' we prevent God from delivering us. God is omnipotent, but He cannot deliver us if we depend upon other sources of imagined deliverance. It is when we forsake our idols and turn to the living God, that the power of the Infinite can operate on our behalf. When we have 'burnt our boats', and when we have removed all earthly props from beneath us, and when we are helpless and alone except for God, then we prove the truth of the saying: "and it shall be, that he that calls on the name of the Lord shall be saved".

If we trust wholly and solely in God, we are like a tree planted by the waters. When earthly supplies fail, and when those who trust in material sources are in a condition of drought, we are sustained by invisible resources, which are infinite and inexhaustible because they are of God. We become rooted and grounded in the eternal instead of living an ephemeral existence in time and space. We share with God His life, wholeness, health and prime. We are sustained by the very substance of the divine. We enter into the heart of things. We live the eternal life. We breathe the deep inner breath. We think God's thoughts after Him. We live an interior life, making contact with the deep life of the Eternal Spirit, and because of this our life is as deep as the universe, and we draw upon illimitable powers, and are fed by invisible fountains of living water. "Deep calls unto deep," and "the Spirit bears witness with our spirit that we are the children of God."

God, the Only Substance

> *Divine love has sustained you in the past; it is sustaining you now, and will sustain you always and for evermore.*

The truth about each child of God is that he is forever the object of divine solicitude. To the extent that he lives in a realisation of this truth he is protected from danger and evil, is maintained in health, and supplied with all needed substance.

God is the only true substance. Matter, in spite of its apparent solidity, is not substance. Danger, difficulty, lack, all are an appearance, when compared with the true substance - God. So we turn to God, the perfect reality, acknowledging that apart from Him we are nothing, but that with Him (in union) all things are perfect. In union with the true substance, all the perfections of reality become possible to us. But we have to live constantly in the thought or consciousness that God, as reality, is the perfect, and the only substance, and that we as children of God, share all the perfections of wholeness and reality. Nothing is lacking in the life that is in union with reality, for reality is wholeness; and, of course, there is no lack or incompleteness in wholeness.

> *I see you, beloved, as you stand in Him, whole, complete and perfect even as He is whole, complete and perfect. I see you forever loved and cared for; forever established in the One Eternal Substance.*

Chapter Three

God, the Unchanging

Purses which wax not old

Luke 12:33

The teaching of Jesus is that those who seek first (and presumably find) the Kingdom of God and His righteousness shall have every needed material good added to them. When we find the Kingdom, we discover reality, the only true substance.

Discovering the true substance which is the reality that upholds the universe establishes our consciousness in That which truly is and which can never fail, grow less, or decay, and which remains unaffected when outward things fail. Material substance is but a reflection in time and space of the true substance which is eternal.

Therefore, our Lord bids us not to lay up treasures upon earth, but to lay up for ourselves treasures in heaven, where neither moth nor rust doth corrupt, and where thieves do not break through nor steal. He says: "Sell what you have, and give alms; provide yourselves purses which wax not old, a treasure in the heavens that fails not, where no thief approaches, neither moth corrupts". This has a literal meaning as well as a mystical one. It means literally that if we discover reality and the only true substance, then everything necessary for this life is added.

Now is the time to find the real and true so that we become established in that which fails not; for earthly and human systems are cracking and decaying.

Now is the time to remember that our citizenship is in heaven, that we belong to reality, to that eternal substance, compared with which the outward life is but a reflection.

Now is the time also for us to realise our true identity, and to live in the consciousness that we are children of God, and therefore eternally loved and cared for.

God, the One Reality

Because Reality alone is true and real, we will think, speak and act from its standpoint and from that alone.

Before we can think from the plane or realm of reality, we must have some idea of what reality is like. Of course, we know it is perfection, but our ideas of what perfection is may be faulty and inaccurate. It is impossible to define divine perfection, but we know that it must be a wholeness, completeness, poise and balance in which everything is contained, and nothing is left out. It cannot be anything less than a state of wholeness and perfect order, in which everything is contained, but in which everything is in its right place at the right time. To think of reality in this way, even though our ideas may be but crude, is to obey our Lord's injunction to set our affection on things above. To think from the standpoint of the twenty-third Psalm is to think from the standpoint of reality, for this Psalm describes things as they really *are*, and not as they appear. This is reality - all things contained therein and as they really are in a state of perfect order.

Through thinking in harmony with reality we are led to do the right thing at the right time, so that harmony results; whereas, if we think from the standpoint of appearances, we naturally do the wrong thing, thus creating disorder and increasing our suffering.

To think from the standpoint of reality (God's perfection) is to lay up treasures in heaven. It not only transforms our life here, but it builds up the body through which we can function on heavenly planes.

If at any time we are in doubt, we remember that love is the key. If things are difficult and perplexing, then we think, speak and act according to divine love, and lo, behold, the difficulty passes away. When we do this, we think, speak and act in accord with reality.

Chapter Four

God, the Power Within Us

Above all that we ask or think.

Ephesians 3:20

As most of you know, a favourite text of mine is "unto Him that is able to do exceeding abundantly above all that we ask or think, according to the power that works in us". God is able to do great things for us. He, being the only power, is the only one who can do these wonderful things for us, beyond our desires and even our imagination. God, being the creative power of the universe, who has created all that is, is the one who can do for us exceeding abundantly, above all we can ask or think. God the Creator, has the power to create through the long processes of nature, or he can create instantaneously, now at this moment, according to our need. Do we need protection? A legion of angels is instantly available for our succour. Do we need food, or money? It can be supplied abundantly. Do we need life and health? Both can be manifested "out of his riches in glory by Christ Jesus".

And these wonderful things which are above all that we ask or think, are "according to the power that works within us". Not the power of the self, but the power of the indwelling life of God, which in all its infinitude is with us now, in this place, at this moment, in our own soul and being. We look within and find all that we need, because God is there in all His power.

Within you is the power; not the power of a finite personality, which is helpless in itself and bound by the limitations of the sense life, but the power of the infinite, which is the one and only power. At any one point, the whole of the infinite power of God is present and available to the trusting soul. He is *able,* He is *willing,* here and now, in this place, by His indwelling, and by working through us, to do exceeding abundantly, above all we can ask or think.

God's Good Will

Life desires for us only our highest good; it is constantly trying to lead us to higher and better things. Life has a glorious purpose for us, which would be realised in our experience if we would but allow it to do so. Life is a spiritual experience; it is governed by spiritual laws. If we obey the call of the spirit then we are divinely protected, and our wants supplied. So long, however, as we remain in the wilderness of self we are not divinely protected, neither are our needs divinely met, neither are we divinely guided. We can claim divine protection, supply, and guidance only when we have surrendered to the divine will and purpose. When we have surrendered everything to the Lord, then the Lord can deal bountifully with us, and He can cause us to lie down in green pastures, and He can restore our souls and lead us in the paths of righteousness for His name's sake.

Life is perfect; it is we who create our own evil through being out of harmony with it. We still demand our own way, we still desire inwardly even though we do not actually voice it as a prayer: "My way, not Thine, oh Lord". We want God to be our servant and to answer our prayers in order that the desires of self may be ministered to. So long as we do this, we make our life very difficult for ourselves. It becomes filled with discord, evil happenings and fears of worse to come. But when we surrender to the Infinite Wisdom and Love, when our prayer is: "Lead Thou me on," it becomes possible for the Lord of Life to lead us into the only path that is right for us, and which alone can bring us into a state of harmony, order, perfection and good.

We learn to 'trust the current which knows the way', and then we realise that we are eternally loved and cared for, and we find it to be so in our experience.

Chapter Five

God, the Liberator

Man is a spiritual being, living in a spiritual universe, governed by spiritual laws.

Man, the true child of God, is a spiritual being, living in a spiritual universe, governed by spiritual laws. Man enjoys the privileges of a son of God and a denizen of Heaven, the true world of reality, to the extent that he lives in harmony with the laws of heaven. They alone enter into the liberty of the sons of God, who live as sons of God should live. It is not possible to run with the hare and hunt with the hounds. Man can serve only one master. He cannot serve both God and Mammon.

Those whose minds are heavenly, and whose aims are of a heavenly nature, are forever loved and cared for: not out of pity or because of favour, but because they live in accord with the laws of Heaven - laws which can only bring forth results that are harmonious, lovely and good.

To the extent that we live in harmony with Heaven, do we enter into Heavenly liberty. That is to say, to the extent that we love God and our neighbour, instead of ourselves, and seek to give rather than to get, to that extent do we find the life of Heaven expressed in this relative life of this restricted consciousness.

The teaching of Jesus Christ, if followed, leads us into perfect liberty - a liberty that is a protection against poverty, want, danger and disaster. People have thought that they could find, and attain to, this state of liberty, through reading a lot of books, following certain cults, by juggling with their mind, and by following various teachers. But it can be found only through following and putting into practice the actual teaching of Jesus. He shows us how to live according to the rules of Heaven, so that we can manifest a heavenly state here on earth.

The Ability of God

> *(God) is able to do exceeding abundantly.*
>
> Ephesians 3:20

God is able to do for us far more wonderful things than ever we dream of asking or even imagining. God is *able*. He has the ability. He has established an internal principle which never alters or fails, and which, if complied with, can, and always does and will, accomplish the impossible, and do great things, for us, whereof we are glad.

Oh, yes, God is *able*. When we have done all we possibly could, and have failed, and when we leave off trying, God does the impossible, and we are delivered from troubles, difficulties, temptations and habits, that hemmed us in on every side. When we are beaten, and yet trust in God, he then arises in His strength, and puts to flight the enemy.

Yes, God *is* able. His strength is made manifest in our weakness, so that "when I am weak, then I am strong". His victory is made manifest in our defeat. His success appears when we have failed utterly. And it is all for us. He loves us with an everlasting love, and with loving kindness does he draw us. All blessings may be ours, if we will but trust Him, instead of relying upon people, or things, or circumstances.

It is wonderful, wonderful, wonderful what God does for us if we trust Him and withhold nothing; learning to give freely of all that we have of love, substance, and service, relying upon the spirit and divine principle to carry us through. We cannot, however, enjoy God and His provision and the carefree life, if we do not prove Him by daring experiment.

> Bring me all the tithes into the storehouse, that there may be meat in mine house, and prove me now herewith, saith the Lord of hosts, if I will not open you the windows of Heaven, and pour you out a blessing, that there shall not be room enough to receive it.
> Malachi 3:10

CHAPTER SIX

God, the Unfailing

God is our refuge and strength.

Psalm 46:1

When everybody fails us, and when all our own efforts are in vain, and when everything we hold to or depend upon passes from us, and when we feel friendless and alone, still God fails not. It is when we come to the end of all things and are at our extremity, it is then that we discover God, and find Him a very present help in trouble.

At various times in the world's history there have appeared men and women of great, outstanding faith. On examining the story of their life, it is always found that they have passed through great experiences, and that it was in their time of deepest need and apparent failure that they found God to be not only an omnipotent God, but also one who would and could never fail them. They discovered that if they did but trust God, utterly and completely, then God had to do something, because of his very nature and character. They discovered also that so long as they held back ever so slightly, relying on 'self' ever so little, then the action of God did not take place. It was only when they trusted wholly and completely that a wonderful deliverance came.

When all people and things fail us and we are stripped of all things, and we ourselves fail and even our prayers are useless, it is less difficult for us to trust God completely, for the simple reason that there is no one else in whom we can trust - only God remains. This is the object of experiences, simply in order to make it easier for us to discover an *available* God. If we trusted voluntarily instead of clinging to self, such experiences would not be necessary, but if they have been necessary in our case, let us not regard them as evil, but rather give thanks because they have been the means of our finding or discovering God.

Yes, glorious fact, whatever happens, whatever befalls us, God never fails.

Chapter Seven

God, our Help and Inward Power

Give us help from trouble (O God): for vain is the help of man.

Psalm 108:12.

In the above words the Psalmist gives us the secret of divine care and supply. We have not only to seek God as the only one who can deliver and sustain us, but we have also to acknowledge that "vain is the help of man".

When we acknowledge that our own finite efforts are all in vain and also the help of all men, then it becomes possible for us to approach the one power and source of power in the right spirit. This is not the spirit of servility, but of utter dependence upon the spiritual power of reality. We can approach the Infinite only to the extent that we acknowledge our own helplessness and that of any human being. It is when we are right down at bedrock bottom, so to speak, and when there is none who can deliver, it is then, and only then, that we can turn to God in the right manner, so that the action of God can take place.

But we have not only to acknowledge our own helplessness, and the inability of any human being to help us, we have also to turn to the Lord (the one life and source of all life) depending entirely upon the infinite power for whatever it is that we need. When we try to do this, all sorts of wrong ideas may come to us – ideas of things we can do, of plans we can make, of people or human or material resources that we might make use of or depend upon. But these must be ignored or dismissed; for they prevent us entirely from entering into a realisation of truth. As we keep out these wrong ideas, and cast ourselves entirely upon God, acknowledging that the spirit is the sole source of supply, our only guidance and our only protection, we gradually enter into truth. When we do this, we are free. For, "Ye shall know the truth, and the truth shall make you free".

God, the Inward Power

The power that works in us.

Ephesians 3:20.

One of the secrets of divine care is to find the hidden power that supports the universe, and from which all manifestation springs. Man's powers are limited and soon exhausted; also, he finds that the forces of what he calls fate are far too much for him, and that he cannot battle successfully against them. But when he ceases to fight against life, and instead seeks and finds the One Inward Power, he becomes established in the divine order in which is no violence, disorder or evil of any kind.

We make contact with the hidden power through waiting upon God, through staying our mind upon God, and meditating upon truth each day long enough to enter into a state of peace and confidence.

It is helpful to take a definite promise of God, one that especially appeals to us, and to keep reading it, and pondering over it, until a realisation of its truth, and of the fact that it applies to us, as though we were the only son or daughter of God in the world, comes to us. When we reach this stage, we become conscious of unlimited power sustaining us. After this, we have to be careful not to think, write and talk ourselves out of the power. If we think and speak in terms of, say, the twenty-third Psalm, we remain in the power, and it remains in us. But if we talk about ourselves as being sick, or weak, or hard up, or in danger, etc., then we think and talk ourselves out of power into weakness, and into the wilderness, where disorder and dangers of all kinds abound.

In spite of appearances, we must think of God as a loving Father-Mother, and ourselves as children of God, forever loved and provided for, and upheld by heavenly powers.

Chapter Eight

God, the Good

Every good and perfect gift is from above

James I:17.

Divine providence looks after us and sustains us through all eternity; that is, always in the eternal now. As eternal beings, we have never lacked anything throughout eternity and, of course, we never shall. Here we are, in the eternal now, and always have been, and always and forever we are sustained and supported by divine love, life and power. Not one moment has God ever failed this. It is impossible for God to fail us; if He did, we should cease to be. We are 'beings', because we have our being in God. Without God we have no being at all. Because God is, we are, and without Him, we have no life and no consciousness. Because we have life, consciousness, being, we know that God is, for we have no being or consciousness of our own or apart from Him.

We, therefore, live and move and have our being in God. In Him we possess, for 'right uses', everything that is necessary for our spiritual and temporal life. We can no more lack any good thing, really, than an angel in heaven, or even God Himself. We are forever loved and cared for, because our real, interior life, reaches right down into the depth of God, who made heaven and earth.

We are established in the one power and life from which everything springs, and without which nothing could have any life or existence at all. In this infinite and inexhaustible life and substance we find all that we need, and we can find it nowhere else. In the love, power and might of God we are forever protected, sustained and preserved from evil. Because we live and have our being in God, evil is excluded, and only good can come to us, for God is the author of all good, and in Him only good is. Also, because God is good itself, He can only do good and know good.

Finding, then, our refuge in God, and abiding under the shadow of the Almighty, we find ourselves forever loved and cared for, and the recipients of all good and blessing.

Chapter Nine

God, the Rewarder

And whatsoever he does shall prosper.

Psalm 1:3.

The above are the words of Scripture. They are a divine promise that is as true today as it was on the day it was written. It is absolutely true that with the Divine blessing resting upon us and our work, all that we do prospers. The carnal mind tells us that this is not so, and that our prosperity depends upon our cleverness, and that, as we're not very clever; we can never succeed or be prosperous. This untruth has to be combated and countered by truth. In the face of such suggestions, we have to affirm the truth as stated in God's word. In it we are told definitely that the man is blessed whose delight is in the law of Jehovah, and who meditates upon it day and night. The man of God prospers because inwardly he is a spiritual being, with his roots reaching down to the one source of all creative life and power, and he knows it and is conscious of it. Because of this he is guided in all that he undertakes, and though he may make mistakes, these are overruled for good; and prosperity follows him in such a way as to free him from all anxiety and strain.

But whereas those who work apart from God may be prosperous, and often are, there is no blessing in their prosperity. It is wrung from life at great cost of effort and is only retained by fighting for it. In contrast to this how different is the case of the God-man, or man of God. He enjoys the blessing of Jehovah, and with it He addeth no sorrow (Proverbs 10:22). One who finds God in the secret place of the most high, and who draws all his sustenance from heavenly and eternal sources, is conscious of a great joy, and feels that he is being carried along on a stream of blessedness to his highest good.

God the Giver

> *Ask and ye shall receive that your joy may be full.*
> John 16:24.

The love of God never forsakes us. God in His grace and mercy waits to bestow upon us the riches of His Divine bounty, but He does not force them upon us. Instead, we are told to ask and receive, that our joy may be full. The promise does not say that our joy will be partial, but that it shall be full. The promise is unrestricted: it sets no bounds or limits to our joy and satisfaction. We are encouraged to ask great things of God, so that we may receive great blessings. There is no stinting on the part of God. He wants us to ask to be filled, not partly filled, with the greatest amount of the greatest of all possible blessings and good. And further, we are invited to accept the blessings of God as well as to ask for them.

Some of us, alas, never ask God for a blessing: we ignore our one source altogether. Or we may ask, but do not accept; never expecting any reply to our asking. Or, again, we may take all God's blessings as a matter of course: never giving thanks, or uttering praise for all the blessings we receive. The true way to live a life of blessedness is first to recognise that all good and blessing come from the Lord: secondly, to look to the Lord for a blessing, and to ask for it: thirdly, to accept the blessing and to give thanks for it and to praise God for it.

There is also a fourth stage, which is, that we should give. Blessings must not merely be received, they must be used in the service of others, in an endeavour to make them as happy and blessed as we are ourselves. To receive and not to give curses their life; it stops that free circulation which is the secret quality of true life. The wise ask with confidence and receive abundantly; and they also give freely. There are no clutching hands in the life of the spirit, but a free coming and going, an unhampered circulation. This is the essence of true life. Receive abundantly, give freely. Give abundantly, receive freely. If we do our part, the Lord does His part.

God, the Preserver

Goodness and mercy shall follow me all the days of my life.

Psalm 23

David was only stating the bare truth when he gave utterance to the above words. He was saying what is true of everyone who puts his whole trust in God, instead of the arm of flesh. God's plan or purpose concerning our life is perfect, whole, complete. There is nothing left out, there is no need unprovided for, there is no loophole through which disaster can come. The Lord puts a hedge or fence round about us, which protects us from all evil, lack and danger. Nothing can pass through that hedge or fence except by divine permission.

That hedge is preserved so long as we think, live, act and speak according to the divine. When we are in perfect accord with the divine will and purpose, then the divine plan can be revealed in us, and manifested in our life. Divine love is always seeking to give us the highest good, the greatest blessing, the most perfect joy, but we spoil it all by not being in harmony and correspondence with the divine plan or purpose. The divine order and perfection are everywhere present in all their fullness and completeness. There is no lack in the abundance and the fullness of God's provision and bounty. What we have to do is to come into accord and correspondence with the perfect order which is present with us now.

One of the secrets of the care-free life is to recognise that the fullness and abundance of God's bounty are with us at all times in all their completeness; and that the protecting power of the Lord is round about us. God is in the midst of us in all His infinitude and power. Blessed are those that trust in Him.

Chapter Ten

God, our Father-Mother

Call no man your father upon the earth: for one is your Father, which is in Heaven.

Matthew 23:9.

Our Father, who art in Heaven, hallowed be Thy name. Thy Kingdom come, Thy will be done in earth as it is in Heaven. Let Thy Kingdom come in this body of mine, and let Thy will of love, light, and good be done in it, even as it is in the Light body, or the glorious body of the Lord. Let Thy glory fill the temple; let Thy Light fill my body; let Thy presence be known and felt this day, and every day.

Let Thy Kingdom of love, harmony and order be established in my will, and in my life. May I love Thee with my whole heart and regard all fellow humans as my brothers and sisters.

Because Thou art my Father, all is well. I am upheld by divine powers, I am guided in paths of peace and blessedness, and all that I need comes to me just at the right time. My life is filled with blessing, Love attends my way, and all things work together for good.

Because Thou art my Mother, I am a child of God, a spiritual being, inhabiting eternity. Heavenly laws govern my life, and the joy of heaven is my portion.

Because Thou art my Father-Mother, I enjoy Thy peace – the peace of God which passes all understanding; and this garrisons my heart and mind in the love of Christ.

Because I am established in eternity, I live in the eternal now. Always and forever, I am safe in Thy love. None shall pluck me out of my Father-Mother's hand. In every experience of life is divine love, and behind every happening is divine wisdom. Thy love and wisdom, which are infinite, are forever working on my behalf, leading me to my highest good, and seeking to bring me to my highest joy. And so I go forward, with Thee.

> THY LOVE ENFOLDS ME
> THY WISDOM GUIDES ME
> THY POWER UPHOLDS ME

Part 2: God, our Centre and Source

Hamblin Vision Publishing

CHAPTER ELEVEN

One Central Source

Deep down within the most interior part of our being we find the one life, which is self-renewing from within itself, for ever fresh and unimpaired, unchanging and eternal. The one life, with which we are at one, or with which we are identified, renews us moment by moment, and also unites us with all our fellows and with all creatures. Deeply within them we recognise the same one life which also is deeply within our own being. In this blessed unity and oneness we find peace and satisfaction.

One Central Source

Life proceeds from the one central source, for only from life can life come. There is one Infinite life which gives life to all things, and Jesus realised that He was one with that life, and that interiorly He was the life itself. This is the realisation to which we all shall come, for Jesus Christ came to be the first-born of many brethren. "I am come that they might have life, and that they might have it more abundantly". "And this is life eternal, that they might know Thee the only true God (life and the source of life)". That they might *know* the only true God - the One Infinite life and their oneness with it. This *knowing*, or true gnosis, is the great secret which our Lord came to impart. Even as He understood and knew Truth - His oneness with the one life, His very identity with it, so did he seek to help others to a similar state of realisation, so that we all might be one.

His hearers did not understand His message, for Jesus spoke beyond His time. He was as one 'born out of due time', in one sense, yet actually, of course, He came just at the right time. His hearers could not understand Jesus when He said: "I am the bread which comes down from Heaven; he that eats me shall not hunger anymore, or thirst anymore". They did not realise that His words had an interior and mystical meaning.

Later, however, St John, the mystical writer of the mystical fourth gospel, *did* understand. In the first chapter he tells us of the Creative Logos (translated Word), without Whom nothing was made (created) that was made (created). He says further that those who received Him (the Logos) to them gave He power to become the sons of God. They were to be just the same as Jesus was, for they would not be begotten "from blood, nor from natural desire, nor yet from the design of man; but from God Himself" (*Ferrar Fenton's translation*).

What a wonder is life!

Ideas come from the invisible and clothe themselves with suitable atoms which also come out of the invisible. Invisible substance is whipped into a vortex, and Lo, a world is born! There is nothing fixed, everything is fluidic. Atoms come from the invisible and pass back into the invisible. Archetypal ideas remain, but the atoms which clothe these ideas come and go. Manifestations may be fleeting, but the one life remains.

We belong not to time, but to the timeless. We are not the changing scene: we are one with that which sustains and supports it.

CHAPTER TWELVE

God, the Giver of Life

They that wait upon the Lord shall renew (change) their strength.

(Isaiah 40:31)

If we wait upon the Lord, looking ever deeper and deeper within our own soul, we come at last to the one life, which is our true centre, and with which we are one forever.

In this one life, we are one with every living creature. In fact, in our highest moments of realisation it seems as though, in our most interior selves, we are the life which animates all living creatures. We experience a lovely and delicious unity with all creation - the rising of the sun, and the going down of the sun: the birds and animals and other creatures: the flowing and ebbing of tides, the stars coming nightly to the sky.

But this, after all, in spite of being so interior, is only the shell of the great mystery. We go still deeper and find ourselves truly one with the One Source of all. We enter into timelessness; we are in the eternal now. We find ourselves one with That which changes not; we realise that we are established in the Eternal, and that our true life is lived in God.

> *Who we truly are we cannot say; we only know that the Lord has promised to write upon us His new name.*

What we are cannot be defined; we only know that we are one with the *ineffable one* - brought into a state of unity with the Lord of all life by divine grace.

We acknowledge that what has been accomplished is not of ourselves at all. In spite of all our strivings it is all of God, for He is the author and inspirer of all our aspiration. We of ourselves could never know God, neither could we have any desire to seek God. It is only because God is in us (*"ye are the temple of God, and the Spirit of God dwelleth in you"* – 1 Corinthians 3:16), that we have any desire to know God - for only God can know God. It is the Spirit of God in us who knows God.

God immanent gazes, face to face, with God transcendent. The son has returned to his Father, saying: "I and my Father are one".

Chapter Thirteen

God, as Love

"God is Love", said the Apostle John. "Greater love hath no man than this - that a man lay down his life for his friends".

"If divine love be in our heart, then do we see love everywhere". What we give to the world comes back to us an hundredfold. "Judge not and ye shall not be judged, condemn not, and ye shall not be condemned: forgive, and ye shall be forgiven. Give, and it shall be given unto you; good measure, pressed down, and shaken together, and running over, shall men give into your bosom. For with the same measure that you meet withal it shall be measured to you again".

We become engulfed in a great sea of love. Love ministers to us through a hundred or even thousands of different channels. The more we give, the more we receive. In vain we try to give back to life some fraction of the Love which is showered upon us, but all in vain, for the more we try to give, the more do we become overwhelmed by the ministrations of Love. Love pours its blessings upon us with ever-increasing measure. And this is the more overwhelming when we remember that we have no true love of our own, and that the love which makes us pour out our soul in benediction, compassion and mercy upon all mankind, and upon all creation, is not of ourselves, but is the Love of God which has entered our heart and is changing us into its own likeness.

Yes, it is the Love of God in us which makes us love others. We have no love towards God, of our own. It is only because God is within us that we can know God: it is only because Love is within us that we can love God: it is only because of this that we can love mankind and regard our fellow-men with infinite compassion.

Yes, the more we give, the more we receive. The more we empty ourselves, the more we become filled. Every day and several times a day, we should address ourselves, to all the world, in the silence of the soul, and make the following statement:

> *Dear people everywhere, I love you all, I love you.*

God, Our Centre of Blessedness

Instead of the thorn shall come up the fir tree, and instead of the brier shall come up the myrtle tree.
                                       Isaiah 55:13

In our body and circumstances are manifested the thought-patterns in our mind. If our body and affairs are filled with disorders, it is not because it is God's will that we should be diseased or subject to disharmonies, for God's will is good-will and can express only that which is good, beautiful and true. The cause of our disorders is that the thought-patterns of our mind are distorted, and not like the original thought-patterns in the mind of God. God's idea concerning us, held eternally in the mind of God, is perfect wholeness, order and health. God's archetypal ideas are, of course, perfect - they cannot be otherwise - but our ideas, held in our human mind, are distorted and imperfect; hence the disorders which keep manifesting in either our body or affairs, or in both.

What is needed is that we should 'forsake our ways' (our unrighteous ways, ways which are not right) and 'return unto the Lord' (the author of order, harmony, wholeness and peace), so that our thoughts should become like unto God's thoughts, and our ideas like unto God's ideas. If we do this, then our text becomes true in our experience. "Instead of the thorn shall come up the fir tree; Instead of the brier shall come up the myrtle tree." Instead of painful disorders of the body, shall manifest health and wholeness (ease, in place of dis-ease). Instead of disharmonies in our affairs, shall manifest order and blessedness.

> I hold myself in the great silence, pliant and flexible, quiet and receptive, so that God's eternal idea of health and wholeness may possess my mind and find expression in my life.

CHAPTER FOURTEEN

God, our Source of Victory

Thanks be to God, Who gives us the victory, through our Lord Jesus Christ.

1 Corinthians 15:57

If you are tempted to be discouraged because of your lack of success in the new life, do not give way to it, for actually, in spite of apparent failure, you are building better than you know. Your efforts to travel Godwards, although they may appear to have come to nought, have not been in vain. The work of regeneration and transmutation goes on quietly underneath the surface in spite of outward setbacks. Every time that you look Godwards; every time that you pray: "Thy Kingdom come, Thy will be done in earth as it is in Heaven," every time that you overcome discouragement and depression by praising and thanking the Lord for all His mercies - you are brought nearer to the heart of God, and a further advance is made in the Divine Alchemy within.

Great and extensive changes take place within before there are any signs of improvement without. If we keep our face turned towards the Light, and go forward, even when it may seem that all is lost and that it is useless to try anymore, and if we still turn Godwards in spite of grievous lapses on our part, then all will be well, and nothing can stay our onward march, neither can anything prevent our upward climb.

If in spite of the apparent hopelessness and uselessness of so doing we continue to keep our face turned to the Light, then we are raised up out of our "slough of despond" to higher and better things, and in course of time are ushered into the glorious liberty of the sons of God.

Do not despair. The very fact that you are assailed proves that you are destined to a high estate, and that "power has been given you to become a son of God, born not of blood, nor of the will of the flesh, nor of the will of man, but of God." (John 1: 12-13)

> God is my Source of victory

CHAPTER FIFTEEN

God, our Source of Protection

They shall not hurt nor destroy in all my holy mountain.

Isaiah 11:9

The term 'holy mountain' we interpret to mean the higher consciousness. If we really can enter into God-consciousness in which our mind functions in correspondence with the Mind of God, then no evil can hurt or destroy. What we can realise inwardly becomes manifested outwardly.

This may be beyond some of us; but, should this be the case, we can declare in the face of danger and calamity that God controls every circumstance of our life, and that the Lord God Omnipotent reigns.

The important thing is to overcome fear. Fear makes us vulnerable, while fearlessness makes us immune. A fierce dog will bite one who fears him, but he will not bite one who is unafraid of him. By declaring that God controls every circumstance of our life, and also by affirming that the Lord God omnipotent reigns, and also by praying "Thy will be done on earth, as it is in Heaven", we cease to fear.

Such statements of truth as these help us to stay our mind upon God. The result of staying our mind upon God is to enter into God's inward peace. When we enter into God's peace, we have found God, we have realised His presence, and all fear put away. When we have lost all fear in realising God's peace, then no evil can come nigh. "They shall not hurt nor destroy in all My Holy Mountain".

Even though we cannot realise God's peace, yet by declaring the Truth about God, and by affirming God's presence, power and reality, our mind can be fortified in God, after which harmony and order will follow.

> I put my trust in God, who is the only power and presence.

All things begin to work together for good directly we start loving God, although the reverse may seem to be the case. If we love God (the good, the beautiful and the true, also purity, righteousness, order, perfection), then we refrain from evil (the following of which produces suffering and disorder) and think and act with God, instead of against divine law. In other words, if we love God, then we live according to Love's decrees; and this, of course, can bring only harmonious results.

Directly we depart from love we create disorder; but directly we begin to think and act according to Love, then harmony begins to be created, and finally will manifest. Everything works according to divine law; if it were not so the universe would smash itself up. The basic law of life is love; consequently, if we live according to love, by loving God and our neighbour then we enter into the divine harmony and order.

All things work together for good to them that love God.
Romans 8:28

Everything comes to pass at the right time if we do our part, which is simply to love God with all our mind and strength and our neighbour as ourselves. For, as St John says, if we do not love our brother whom we have seen, how can we love God whom we have not seen?

The essential thing, then, is that we should love in the divine way, pouring out our soul in blessing and benediction and mercy and compassion. Then we come into the stream of life and are carried along on a stream of blessedness to our highest good, "while all the divine forces hasten to minister to our eternal joy."

> Because I love God, all things are working together for good.

Chapter Sixteen

God, our Source of Stability

God is not moved, though all things be passing.

We enter into a state of genuine stability when we realise that the eternal God changes not, and that all things (done according to His will) come to pass at the right time.

The beginner thinks feverishly that he has got to alter things, and that he must spend a considerable part of his time in imploring God to alter his mind and change his purpose. But the more experienced pilgrim desires only to allow things to come to pass, according to the Mind of God.

"It has been my experience," writes a pilgrim, "that everything in the divine economy comes to pass at the right time, and that God overrules everything for good." This is eternally true. What is essential is that we should desire only that the will of God should be done, and that we should look to God alone for all that we need, recognising that God controls every circumstance of our life.

It was said of George Muller: "Times might be bad, financial panic might be abroad, but the stream of gifts failed not – yea, rather became stronger. It was as though, as a donor once remarked, the institution lay hidden under the shadow of the Almighty from the stress of the age".

Yes, if we were to depend upon man, we should be affected by all the change to which man is subjected. But if we depend wholly upon God, then we become one with the Changeless and altogether Dependable One. Consequently, we are but little affected by the changes and upheavals of life.

Those who stay their mind upon the *changeless one* are upheld by invisible powers belonging to the Eternal. If we stay our mind upon God, day and night, then, to quote the first Psalm, we become like "a tree planted by the rivers of water, that brings forth his fruit in his season; his leaf also shall not wither; and whatsoever he does shall prosper."

> My mind is stayed on the Changeless One.

CHAPTER SEVENTEEN

God, our Source of Substance

When my father and my mother forsake me, then the Lord will take me up.

Psalm 27:10

When all earthly resources fail and friends forsake us, or are removed from us, then the Lord, the one power, substance and presence, sustains us.

Life's experiences are designed to bring us into a state of cosmic awareness, in which we know inwardly, by direct knowing, i.e. by an interior awareness, that all our needs are eternally supplied from the one central creative centre. In this state of inward and pure knowing we realise that interiorly everything in our life is divinely ordered and arranged, that everything comes to pass at the right time, just like the rising of the sun each morning and the coming of the stars to the evening sky.

When we realise this great truth, we enter into peace and enjoy such a feeling of certainty as no pen can describe. Also, things in our life begin to drop into the right place in a wonderful manner.

The old nature, however, finds it easier to trust in the Mammon of Unrighteousness than in the invisible powers which maintain the worlds. It finds it easier to trust in silver and gold than in the inspired statement of Paul: "My God shall supply all your need out of His riches in glory by Christ Jesus."

Our affairs may appear to be in a parlous state, while any deliverance according to worldly standards may seem to be quite impossible. Yet if, when everything else fails, we fall back upon God, trusting Him entirely, then the impossible is proved to be possible. When we realise that everything comes to pass at the right time and that God controls every circumstance of our life, then our affairs begin to mend and we learn another lesson of entire dependence upon God, the invisible sustainer and deliverer.

> Everything that I need comes to me at the right time.

God, the Source of Holy Breath

The Spirit breathes where it will, and you hear its voice.
John 3:8

There is a breathing of the spirit, just as there is a breathing of the physical lungs. In the same way that this outward body breathes air, so is it possible for the awakened soul to breathe the finer aethers of the breath of God.

It is through this inward breathing that the soul draws upon God for its sustenance, and the inward life of man is nourished and developed.

When we enter into a state of realisation, we know what this breathing of the spirit is, for, without any trying on our part, we find that our breathing has become as deep as the universe. Not only has it become deep, indescribably so, but also it has become conformed to an inward rhythm, so that we breathe in correspondence with the spirit, and with the whole universe.

This slow, deep and holy breath of the spirit begins with a slight gasp, something like the sort of sob which people give after they have been holding their breath while gazing at some exciting incident. After this catching of the breath, the breathing then proceeds deeply, smoothly, rhythmically, controlled by the spirit and not by ourselves.

Then it is that we enter the great silence. Disturbing noises fade into the distance, and the peace of God flows through us like a river.

No attempt should be made to slow down the breathing. We strongly advise against any such attempt. The real breathing comes to us naturally, as a result of our concentration upon God, our divine centre.

Then the Gospel of John goes on to say: "So is everyone that is born of the spirit". Through being born of the spirit, we also breathe in the same way as the one spirit. "The spirit itself bears witness with our spirit, that we are the children of God", by means of the Holy Breath.

> Blissfully, I breathe in harmony with the Spirit.

God, Source of Life and Light

The prayer of faith shall save the sick; and the Lord shall raise him up.

James 5:15

Prayer is returning to the Lord of life and light and becoming at one with Him. By the term 'Lord' is meant not the human Jesus, but the resurrected, risen and glorified Christ, victorious over every limitation.

To pray in this way is to *see* with our spiritual sight, or eye of faith, the Lord's body of glory. This is not of ordinary matter but is composed of eternal light substance. It can know no decay, age or deterioration. It vibrates at a higher rate than matter and is glorious beyond description.

To *see* the Lord's glorious body is to realise a state of perfection and beauty far beyond all human words and powers of description. We begin to realise what wholeness really means; what perfect health actually is; what permanence and indestructibility really are.

As we think of the Lord's glorious body, we envisage light and glory, beauty and wholeness, glory and perfection. We do not visualise what we want to see, but we become raised through prayer until it is granted us to see and realise something of the glory of the risen body of light and everlasting substance of the Lord.

> And we beheld His glory, the glory as of the only begotten of the Father, full of grace and truth.
>
> John 1:14

Our text goes on to say further that "the Lord shall raise him up". If man prays aright, and prays often and fervently, then the Lord raises him up. This is generally understood to mean that he will be raised up from his bed of sickness; but it is true also that the Lord raises us up to a higher consciousness, where we can see that which is not lawful for the ordinary consciousness to know anything about.

We have to become changed before we can see the Lord. We can become changed only by constant prayer. As we become changed, so do we become raised up, and as we become raised up, so do we see the Lord.

> Through turning to the Lord of life and Light, I become one with Him.

Chapter Eighteen

God, our Rock

For in the time of trouble He shall hide me in His pavilion: in the secret of His Tabernacle shall He hide me; He shall set me up upon a rock.

Psalm 27:5

This text becomes true in our experience to the extent that we can take our stand in the eternal and make Him our refuge and fortress. The greater our conception of God the more completely is He able to hide us "secretly in a pavilion from the strife of tongues."

If we make continual contact with God our divine centre, and if we trust Him entirely, taking His promises to mean what they say, then He is able to fulfil his promises. God is the same, He does not change. The same power is available to us today as in the day of the apostles, or the patriarchs. All that is required is that we should trust God as in days of old. "All things are possible to them that believe". The power of God is unlimited; it is only our lack of faith and trust that can limit it.

Of Hudson Taylor, founder of the China Inland Mission, it was said:

> He has seen God, in answer to prayer, quell the raging of the storm, alter the direction of the wind, and give rain in the midst of prolonged drought. He has seen Him, in answer to prayer, stay the angry passions and murderous intentions of violent men, and bring the machinations of his people's foes to nought. He has seen Him, in answer to prayer, raise the dying from the bed of death, when human aid was in vain: has seen Him preserve from the pestilence that walks in darkness, and from the destruction that wasted at noonday. For more than eight years and a half he has proved the faithfulness of God in supplying his own temporal wants and the needs of the work in which he has been engaged.

It is ever thus. To the extent that we trust God and put Him to the test, God becomes to us an available God.

> God hides me in His secret pavilion, from the strife of tongues.

God, Our Invisible Power

> *They shall not be ashamed in the evil time: and in the days of famine, they shall be satisfied.*
>
> Psalm 37:19

Our text speaks of the righteous or upright - those who live their life in God, whose trust is in God, and whose sole hope is in God. Those whose life is rooted in passing and material things find themselves without resources in the day of adversity. But those whose life is rooted in unchanging reality, who are unified with the one substance and who are filled with the one life, these are sustained and supported by invisible powers in the evil day, so that adversity does not affect them.

When times are prosperous and life is easy for all, the unbeliever scoffs at the righteous and thinks he is a fool. But when the 'evil time' comes it is another story. The scoffer finds that he has no means of support, and that he has to go just wherever life and the forces of disorder may push or drag him. Struggle as he may, he finds himself at the mercy of powers he does not understand, and which are beyond his control.

But in the case of the godly it is different, for he realises that his life is as deep as the universe and that he is fed from inexhaustible fountains. Neither the evil time nor the day of famine can affect him, or but slightly. His needs are always supplied, and every day provision is made for him.

> Apparent lack will not affect us, for we are fed by inexhaustible fountains, and "all the Divine Forces hasten to minister to us."

God, Our Support

Nothing before,
nothing behind:
The steps of faith
Fall on the seeming void,
and find the rock beneath.

– John Greenleaf Whittier.

A common question is: "Why is it, now that I am trying to live a life of faith, I am being so severely tested?" The answer is, of course, that we can never learn really to know God and enter into freedom without experiencing what Whittier describes in his poem. With nothing before, and nothing behind, and with only the (seeming) void under our feet, we have to make the supreme venture, or act of trust, and step out into the unknown. Then, as our Quaker friend says, we "find the rock beneath".

We should never be able to "find the rock beneath" if we did not trust God and step out into the unknown, on to the seeming void.

GOD THE SOURCE OF GOOD

It is through this terrific experience that we pricked the bubble of illusion, thus finding God and entering into the truth of our being.

It is the same with the everlasting arms. We all know the text: "The eternal God is our refuge; and underneath are the everlasting arms". But this can be of no practical use to us if we have not tested it and proved it by experience. We can never *know* the everlasting arms if we do not *find* them. Also, we cannot find them if we do not do something in order to prove that they are underneath us. But we are afraid to do this. We want to hang on like a drowning man to a rope: we are afraid to let go and trust our all to God. We are afraid to lean back, to fall back, if need be, into the abyss. But if we do trust our all to God, leaning back, even falling back, into the unknown, then we find that we have fallen into the arms of God, and that the everlasting arms are indeed a reality, and that they can never fail.

Then it is that we experience and enjoy true luxury - the luxury of lying in the arms of God. This is true bliss - the bliss which alone can satisfy the longing of the soul. Then it is that we enter into true liberation and freedom. We *know* the truth, and the truth makes us free.

> Trusting God, I find Him.

It is said of Campbell Morgan that in a sermon the title of which was *Our God is a Consuming Fire*, he suggested that what was bliss and heaven to the one who was attuned to it might be hell and torment to one who was not attuned to it.

When I was young, I could never understand how it was that God was said to be love, yet on other occasions He was described as committing people to hell and torment. This dual nature of God baffled me, until I realised that there was no dual nature at all, but that God is always love and can never be otherwise.

When I realised that the same love which gave bliss to those attuned to it must of necessity produce anguish in those who were out of tune and in conflict with it, my heart was satisfied. It was satisfied because I saw that it was not the love vibrations which caused the anguish, but the being out of tune.

If a sinner were put amongst a number of saints, he would be uncomfortable and would long to escape from their midst. This would not be due merely to their conversation, but rather to their soul emanations. Such high vibrations would cause acute discomfort to one who is attuned to the conversation of a taproom.[1]

This revelation or realisation brought joy and peace to my soul, for it cleared God of my suspicions of His character. At once I could see that all our troubles were due to a departure on our part from divine love.

---

1. A bar or pub.

The way of the spirit is harmony and peace, simply because the way of the spirit is love. Love (the Christ-Love) is the key to every situation in life. If we apply love, then all our troubles and disorders become resolved, and we enter into the divine order.

> Let Love consume all the dross.

God of All Harmony

For with the same measure that you mete withal it shall be measured to you again.

Luke 6:38

Jesus came to reveal to us a better way of life. If we follow His teaching, we find ourselves living a life of freedom and joy such as those who follow the path of self-interest can never know.

Jesus taught the principle of absolute justice. What we give, we receive back again. We should not spend our time in begging God to protect us but should live our life in such a way that all life, both visible and invisible, would seek to serve us and minister to us.

"As ye would that men should do to you, do ye also to them likewise" (Luke 6:31). If we follow this injunction, and make it the rule of our life, we find that we are kept away from disorder and dissension and guided into the ways of peace.

One person may be always running into trouble. There are rows, disputes, and even fights, wherever he goes. Another person may cover the same ground and do the same job, and meet with kindness, goodwill and peaceful conditions everywhere. The reason is to be found in their respective states of mind. One is antagonistic, while the other is friendly. One is connected, by the nature of his thoughts, with all the infernal forces of disorder and disruption. The other is connected, also by his thoughts, with all the divine forces which make for harmony, beauty and peace.

The old idea of begging and praying to God for favours is passing away. We do not want favours, neither are they necessary, for life is so perfect that if we only obey its laws (its basic law is love) then everything works together for good. This is infinitely better than begging for favours. St. Paul said: "All things work together for good to them that love God". And Jesus said that we must not only love God, but also our neighbour, that is, our fellow-man. Also, He added, on this one commandment hang all the law and the prophets.

Although we do not beg for favours, we are greatly helped. If we try to love, universally and impartially, then love is showered upon us from a thousand directions. If we try to pray, then the Holy Spirit teaches us how to pray, and turns our feeblest utterances and aspirations into prayers that bring our mind into harmony with the Mind of God.

> I send out love universally and impartially.

Chapter Nineteen

God, our Source of Health

I thank thee, Lord, for life, and health, and wholeness and joy.

If we lack any good thing, we can bring it into manifestation if we only thank and praise God for it sufficiently. The reason why this is so is that thanksgiving and rejoicing tend to change us into the likeness of that which we praise, so that the lack is made good automatically. If we thank the Lord for life, health, wholeness and joy, then the concept of these desirable states is formed in the mind, and we experience a feeling of life, health and wholeness, and we also become filled with joy. If we experience an inward feeling that we are healed, then we find that we are healed.

Of course, it is no use pretending or trying to make ourselves believe what we know is not true; neither is it of any use trying to feel what we do not feel, really and truly. Attempts at self-deception are both harmful and futile. If, however, we thank the Lord, with real gratitude, love and praise, then something takes place within which fills us with joy and peace, and which takes away all fear. We cannot heal ourselves, but thanksgiving opens us to receive an influx of life of a higher quality. Also, we tend to become like that which we meditate upon. Therefore, if we meditate upon our inward limitations, then we grow like them and manifest them; while if we meditate upon life, health, wholeness and joy, then we tend to manifest them outwardly.

But beyond all this there is something else, which is, that deep within our being, right at the very centre, we become conscious of the presence of the Lord Himself. Then the prayer: "Heal me, O Lord, and I shall be healed" takes on a new meaning and significance. It is as though we hear Him say in response: "I *will* heal you and deliver you from every limitation." Then is our heart filled with joy and our soul with thankfulness.

> Thy presence heals me.

In the Epistle to the Hebrews, we are told in chapter eleven that Moses endured what he endured, as seeing *him* who is invisible. But in Ferrar Fenton's translation we are given: "He was equally assured of the unseen as of the seen". This is a free rendering which is not supported by any other modern translator of note, but it probably conveys what the writer to the Hebrews wished to convey. While dealing with outward disorder, Moses was aware of the interior order. He refused to bow to the obvious might and power of Pharaoh, because he was aware of the invisible presence of the King of Kings, Lord of Lords, and only Ruler of Princes.

We belong both to the visible and the invisible. Outwardly, by means of our material body, we make contact with a material world. Inwardly, through the medium of our spiritual body, we inhabit Heavenly spheres.

Thus, we live in two worlds at one and the same time. Just as our material lungs breathe the air around us, so also does the soul "breathe the sweet aethers blowing of the breath of God". Even as the children of Israel ate manna in the wilderness, so also does the soul eat of the heavenly manna.

But if Moses was aware of the unseen, St. Paul was even more so. He was splendidly alive to the fact that we possess a spiritual or celestial body which enables us to function on spiritual or celestial planes. He declared that the unseen is the real, while the seen is but temporal. He said that our citizenship is in Heaven, and that here we have no continuing city.

As we travel along our pilgrim journey we become increasingly aware of the unseen, and also we become increasingly aware of the presence of the angelic hosts. It is a great privilege that we can become aware of our angelic companions, even as the shepherds did at the time of advent, although in a more interior way. We employ no psychic vision, neither do Immortals (angels) take upon themselves a material form for our benefit; but, interiorly, soul touches soul, and we enter into great peace and bliss.

Chapter Twenty

God, our Source of Abundance

Enlarging the boundaries of our mind.

We need to exercise a greater faith, to push back the boundaries of our mind, and enter into a richer, fuller and more abundant life of joy, overcoming and victory; of abundance, happiness and joy.

Elsewhere I have said (probably echoing what someone else has written) that we can go to the ocean of God's limitlessness with a teacup, consequently obtaining only a teacup full of blessing; or we can go to the same ocean with a bucket and take a bucketful. It makes no difference to the limitless as to whether we take a teacup or a bucket, but it makes a great difference to us. God's inexhaustibleness cannot be exhausted or reduced in any way. The infinite cannot become less than infinite. Lack is simply the product of the human mind, or rather, is due to a limitation of the human mind. If we could but remove the barriers, then our life would partake of infinite resources.

But although it may not be possible for us to remove the barriers of our mind, yet it is possible to push them back so as to enlarge our horizons. Instead of praying in limited terms, we can pray in terms of the limitless. God wants to bless us far more than we want to be blessed. Life wants to shower upon us all God's richest blessings, and in fact is always doing so; but, alas, we are not attuned to them, and therefore are not conscious of them.

There is a more excellent way than that of toil and struggle. This more excellent way is to hold in the creative imagination a concept of perfection, beauty, harmony, order and good, and to do so every day without fail. When this is done a feeling of deep and blissful peace comes to the soul, and also the breathing becomes deep and attuned to an interior rhythm.

> I hold in my mind a concept of God's Perfect Good.

God of True Prosperity

> *This book of the law shall not depart out of thy mouth; but thou shalt meditate therein day and night, that thou mayest observe to do according to all that is written therein: for then thou shalt make thy way prosperous; and then thou shalt have good success.*
>
> Joshua 1:8

In Dr. Pierson's *Life of George Muller of Bristol*, we are told that three times in Holy Scripture we find a divine prescription for true prosperity. The first is given above. The second is to be found in Psalm I, while the third is in St. James I:25. "Whoever looks into the perfect law of liberty and continues (i.e. continues looking) meditating on what he there beholds, lest he forget the impression received through the mirror of the Word), this man shall be blessed in his deed". Each text speaks of God's Law and the necessity of meditating upon it. If we think and meditate upon the Law of the Lord, instead of thinking of and brooding over our limitations, we enter into liberty. "The Law of the Lord is perfect, restoring the soul" (Psalm 12). This perfect Law of God, called by St. James the perfect Law of Liberty, is always present, always operating and always ready to bless us. It is the opposite of the appearance of limitation which we see all around us. If we are faced by seeming lack or penurious circumstances, then the remedy is to meditate upon God's perfect law of abundance until we feel set free in spirit, and all our fears set aside. If we meditate upon the divine law of abundance until we *feel* its reality and truth, and are able to realise that "all the divine forces are ministering to us," and every needed blessing is not only coming to us just at the right time, but is also seeking us out, and pursuing us, so to speak, then our outward life will begin to express or manifest that which we have realised inwardly. Not only are we blessed, but we are also filled with joy and peace and blissful feelings which come to us from larger and higher and more Heavenly spheres, to which we really belong. Therefore, we can fall to blessing and praising God with great thankfulness and delight, because we know that our prayer is answered most gloriously, even though we may not have a penny to our name.

> God is prospering the work of my hands.

God of Effortless Action and Achievement

Bear ye one another's burdens and so fulfil the law of Christ.

Galatians 6:2

There are some who, while they cannot do what is called Work of National Importance,[1] owing perhaps to advanced age, or it may be to other duties which take up most of their time, yet are helping more than they know. Indeed, they are helping in such a vital way that when viewed from the spiritual side it is seen that their work is more important than that of the greatest in the land.

---

1. Work of National Importance (WNI) was offered as an alternative to military service for conscientious objectors (COs) during wartime to avoid imprisonment, especially during the two World Wars. This was often farm work, forestry or civilian manual work.
https://history.blog.gov.uk/tag/work-of-national-importance/

The latter render valuable service in the seen and temporal, i.e. the world of effect, whereas the former work in the unseen, or the realm of causation.

This work in the unseen or causal world, in which prayer and thought are brought to bear on the base or source of events, is the most difficult thing possible. It is easy in comparison to be active, in an exterior way, to work long hours and to bear heavy burdens. Indeed, most people are willing to undertake such tasks and burdens, and even to work 25 hours a day, if such a thing were possible. But as for working in the unseen, they will not even think of it, far less attempt it.

Yes, they are right. Such work is not for the many, but only for the few. As a rule, it is not taken up by choice. One does not sit down and say: "Now I will work in the unseen for the salvation of the world." Generally, it happens in this way: a feeling of anguish and a cloud of desolation come down on one. It is the cloud of the suffering of the peoples of the world which comes to us because of our sympathy with the downtrodden and despairing. When this takes place, one does not give way to it, but one works to overcome it by a realisation of truth. We take upon ourselves the burden of the world's woe, and then we work through it until at last we find again God's inward peace, and enter into the light once more, being filled with heavenly joy and divine bliss.

When this is accomplished, we have rendered the highest service that anyone can render, for we have set in motion the silent powers of omnipotence.

> By staying my mind on God, I find inward peace.

God of the Inner Kingdom

The Kingdom of God is within you.

Luke 17:20

Yes, the Kingdom of God is within us - the Kingdom of life, health, wholeness, perfection and joy. When the disciples of John the Baptist were sent to Jesus to ask if he were the Messiah, they were told to take back this answer: "the blind receive their sight, and the lame walk, the lepers are cleansed, and the deaf hear, the dead are raised up and the poor have the gospel (of the Kingdom) preached unto them". Because of these things it was proved that Jesus was from God, and that His work was to bring the Kingdom of God to earth by showing men how to find it within themselves. The Kingdom of God is not a dark kingdom of disease, sickness, ill-health and misery, but is a kingdom of light and health, wholeness and joy.

And so, if we would be healed, we must look within and not into a brazen sky. Yes, inside us we find the Inner Kingdom where God dwells, and if we truly find Him we shall become like Him. "Look unto me, and be ye saved, all the ends of the earth". By 'saved', I take the meaning to be made whole or restored to the divine likeness and image from which we have departed.

We cannot do it of ourselves - that is, we cannot of our exterior selves make ourselves whole. We can become whole only by surrendering to the one who is wholeness itself and who is to be found deep within us, like a lighted candle hidden under a bushel measure.

Jesus said that we should not hide our light under a bushel, but that we should place it on a candlestick, so as to give light to all who come in. By this is meant that we should search inwards and seek diligently until we find the Inward Light, after which it will shine through us, thus helping to bring light to a dark world. Instead of manifesting the darkness of disease or sickness, we are to show forth the light of health and joy.

> Let the inner light be made manifest through me.

God, Whose Nature is Love

> *But the greatest of all these is charity.*
> 1 Corinthians 13:13

The word translated as 'charity' in the Authorised and as 'love' in the Revised versions, respectively, of the New Testament, really means love of a divine nature, which desires only to serve and to bless, to give and to minister, desiring and hoping for nothing in return. It is the reverse of natural love, so-called, which seeks to possess, and which wants to be loved in return. It is not understood by the natural man, for he is self-centred. As Madame Guyon says in *A Method of Prayer*, "the language of love is barbarous to him who loves not but is very natural to one who loves." Yes, one who learns to love according to the way of the divine nature does so as naturally as breathing. He feels that he must pour out all that he has and is upon others; to give himself to the uttermost, without any hope or thought of reward. This alone can give him any real satisfaction. It is only when he gives himself and pours out his soul in constant benediction that he feels at all satisfied.

The result of all this (although he seeks no benefit) is that he becomes a friend of every living thing, both visible and invisible. He is the universal lover who is loved in return by every form of life, both visible and invisible. All the invisible forces welcome him into their habitations, for he loves every creature and is a universal friend.

Wherever he goes love meets him and greets him, and even in the hour of extremity all the invisible Forces seek to minister to him.

Instead of having to fight for and strive after the things that he needs, and which he would have to hold by force were he able to secure them, they all come to him of their own accord, and seek to find him and to bless him.

Yes, the way of true love is the way of harmony and peace, of effortless achievement, of blessing and all things added.

But this is true only of those who seek no reward and who are prepared to lose all things for love's sake. For whoso will lose his life shall save it, while he who would save his life shall lose it. What we hold, we lose. What we give, we gain.

> All that I have and am I give to the world.

Part 3: God the Infinite Good

Hamblin Vision Publishing

Chapter Twenty-One

The Infinite Good

Foreword

Jesus came to teach us a new way of life. He called his gospel the gospel, or good news, of the Kingdom. He said: "Change your minds, for the Kingdom of Heaven approaches" or is near. Then He proceeded to demonstrate that the Heavenly state is the true state for man. The Heavenly state is not disease, sickness, disorder, violence and penury, but health, wholeness, order, peace, harmony and abundance of all manner of good, without a care for the morrow.

The teaching that God sends disease and sickness in order to make us into saints found no place in the gospel of Jesus. Neither did He teach that to be poor and penurious was a sign of holiness. What He did teach was a state of entire freedom from the thraldom of mammon, a state of attainment to liberty and freedom in which every righteous need is abundantly met.

Freedom from want and lack: freedom from the cares of worldly possessions: freedom from all fear of the future, from all care, from all anxiety.

When mankind pays heed to this teaching, and also puts it into practise, then will dawn the day when the whole Creation, and not man only, will enter into liberty and freedom.

When all men depend upon God for supply, realising that their needs will always be adequately supplied, then there will be no robberies (for why should anyone rob another; it would be absurd), and also no murders for the sake of robbery, no quarrels over wills, no wars of aggression, because there will be nothing to be gained by aggression. In fact, the world will become entirely changed, to the extent that mankind adopts the method of Jesus.

> *Change your minds; for the Kingdom of Heaven approaches.*
> Matthew 4:7 (Ferrar Fenton)

> *And do not adapt yourself to this age; but be transformed by the renewal of the mind, to search out what is the intention of God - the good, and noble, and perfect!*
> Paul, the Apostle - Romans 12:2 (Ferrar Fenton)

God the Infinite Good

Our God is just what we believe Him to be. By this I do not mean that what we think can make any difference to reality or the absolute, for the absolute, of course, is beyond all thought and every human concept. What I mean is this, that God, being infinite in all directions, is, *to us*, just what we think Him to be. For instance, if we believe that our God is helpless and unable to govern this world, it follows that our God is just as impotent as we believe Him to be. Because God is infinite in all directions it follows that if we were to believe Him to be capable of governing His own world and delivering His people, that we would find that our God has grown and become all that we believed Him to be. We would find that our God was quite capable of governing His world and able to do what is called the impossible.

Also, if later our idea of God were to grow still greater, then we would find that our God had grown greater in the same measure, and that He was still equal to every demand made upon him.

It seems strange that so many cannot understand this, and that they should continue to grope about in the twilight of unbelief, instead of stepping out into the full-orbed day of faith in an available God.

In early times and in the case of savage races the idea about God was that He was an evil spirit who was responsible for all their diseases and bad luck. They believed that evil plagues and punishments could be staved off only by blood sacrifice which they offered to their God or gods in order to appease his or their wrath. This sacrifice consisted of their own sons and daughters – their first-born. This practise was not confined to the pagans or heathen: it was also common in Israel. *The Temple Dictionary of the Bible* (page 684) says: "There can be little doubt that this terrible custom (of sacrificing their own first-born) was not due to a desire to give the Deity the best, but to a widespread belief in the jealousy of The Deity, who could thus be appeased." Later this practice gave way to the use of animals for sacrifice instead of their first-born sons and daughters. Those who like to do so may read Exodus 22:29. These are supposed to be God's words, but we know very well that Moses must have been mistaken, in the same way that Abraham was mistaken in thinking that God wanted him to offer his son, Isaac, as a blood sacrifice, and David that the Lord had told him to massacre the men, women and children who were unfortunate enough to fall into his hands.

These things are mentioned in order to show that in twilight times the idea of God was that He was jealous and spiteful, and that His wrath could only be appeased by the offering of blood sacrifices.

This idea persisted down the ages; and even in the present day it still lingers. But this is due to the fact that in some quarters the true character of God is still misunderstood.

This idea of appeasing an angry, jealous and a spiteful God by means of sacrifices and gifts should have come to an end with the appearance of Jesus Christ. He taught an entirely different doctrine. He said that the chief characteristic of God is that He is a God of love, not of jealousy and anger; And also, He told his disciples that God was not only His Father in Heaven, but that He was their Father in Heaven, also. He also taught that our Father in Heaven is perfect, and that, we, too, were to be perfect also.

Now that our idea of God has changed for the better, we find that God is all that we believe Him to be. And if we could believe still better of Him, we should find again that He was equal to our highest demands upon Him, because His goodness is infinite.

Divine good will manifest to the extent that we believe God to be Infinite Goodness. As our belief in the goodness of God increases, so will the Divine Good become increasingly manifest. God, being Infinite Divine Goodness, it only needs an increase in our belief and faith, in order to bring Divine Good into action. Goodness infinite awaits manifestation. It is our lack of belief, together with our lack of appropriation, that keeps it back and starves our life.

The teaching of Jesus has revolutionised our ideas about God. We see now that God is Absolute Goodness. Not merely the relative good that we know as being the opposite of relative evil, but the Absolute of Good, which is something infinitely higher, which is a state of wholeness, completeness and perfection such as we cannot describe. We see now that the awful things which in the Old Testament were attributed to the anger and fury of God, were really due to the love of God and to His Perfect Law of Order. So long as the Children of Israel lived according to the Divine order they prospered. It was only when they wandered away from it that

GOD THE SOURCE OF GOOD

they fell on evil times. Jesus taught that God extends his goodwill to all, equally. He does not bestow His good upon some and send evil upon others.

> Ye have heard it has been said, thou shalt love thy neighbour and hate thine enemy. But I (Jesus) say unto you, Love your enemies, bless them that curse you, do good to them that hate you, and pray for them which despitefully use you and persecute you; that ye may be the children of your Father which is in Heaven; for He makes His sun to rise on the evil (person) and on the good (person); and sends rain on the just, and on the unjust.
>
> Matthew 5:43-48

From this we see that the good and the evil person and the just and the unjust have God's blessing showered upon them. God is not good to one and evil to another. He is the same to both. But, while the life of the one who is in harmony with the All Good is blest, the life of the one who departs from the divine order appears to be punished or afflicted. But this is due to being out of correspondence with the divine good. We are not punished *for* our sins: we are punished *by* our sins. If we depart from our centre (the centre and source of all harmony and blessedness), we meet with all manner of disorders and adversities; but directly we get back to our divine centre, order and harmony become restored

This new life of the spirit, or life of regeneration, into which we have entered, is like floating down a stream. So long as we keep in the middle of the stream all goes well. But if we allow ourselves to drift away from it to the edges of the stream, we find ourselves entangled in various obstructions and obstacles so that it is impossible to make any progress. The remedy, of course, or rather, the preventative, is that we should keep to our divine centre, making contact with it by means of constant prayer. Not by saying prayers, but by turning the heart to the Lord within, in praise, thanksgiving, adoration and thankfulness.

Whereas in past times the great evil was in thinking that God was dual - a God of mercy and compassion sometimes, and of anger and fury at others - there is a more insidious evil, which has been the cause of more disease and sickness than can be estimated.

Its first form was really a logical outcome of the belief that God was a jealous deity who had to be appeased, instead of a God of love who was always anxious that we should enjoy His love. This was the teaching of hell and everlasting damnation. When I was young this teaching was giving way before the light of a better understanding of God, but it still held the field in most churches and chapels. It was the practise of preachers then literally to shake their hearers over the brink of hell, and to threaten them with the most awful torments which would continue everlastingly. Unfortunately, there are teachings today which still include this dreadful doctrine of everlasting punishment.

The fruits of this teaching are to be found in the form of sickness and ill-health. Deep down within the subconscious mind is an awful fear of God, which is the cause of an anxiety which is none the less harmful for being repressed. When such sufferers learn that this teaching is erroneous, they enter into a sense of freedom and happiness such as they have never experienced before.

One reader wrote to me once saying that she had always been afraid to pray, "Thy will be done", for fear that God would cast her into Hell!

God, of course, does not cast us into hell, but we ourselves can cast ourselves into outer darkness by rejecting God and deliberately working against the divine good. We are all invited to the feast of divine love, not one is omitted or forgotten. If, however, we refuse the invitation, preferring to remain outside, it is we who cast ourselves out, and not God.

Also, even if we were to do this, it does not follow that we should remain always in outer darkness. The state of darkness may be everlasting, because it must always be the case that those who depart from God put themselves out of the divine light. If we are separate from the light, then we abide in darkness. This does not necessarily mean, however, that we must abide forever in the darkness of separation. The *state* may be permanent, but it is unthinkable that souls should continue to remain everlastingly in that state.

There is always a healing process at work. If we cut our finger, immediately numberless white corpuscles set to work to repair the damage. Nature always seeks to heal us if we need healing. The natural law extends to the spiritual world. It is only reasonable that the same healing process should apply to souls, and that when the anguish of separation from God causes the soul to long for higher things, that its longing for God should be satisfied.

Some readers may say: "What about the parable of Dives and Lazarus?" This is certainly a solemn warning to those who exploit the poor, and live in luxury while others starve, but I cannot think for a moment that God, Who is love infinite, would not allow a truly repentant soul from working its way back to the light. We are drawn nearer to God to the extent that we become like Him. Therefore, as we become changed, and through repentance become more like our Father, it must follow that we are drawn nearer and nearer to the light.

I do not believe that God punishes us at all. We punish ourselves by departing from God's blessedness. "We have erred and strayed from Thy ways like lost sheep. We have followed too much the devices and desires of our own hearts". God is infinite love; consequently, when we do things which are against love, and against our fellow humans, we put ourselves outside the realm of love. And then it follows that the greater the love of God the more severely we hurt ourselves. Love does not hurt us, nor want to hurt us in the slightest degree, for love can only be itself: it cannot be anything different from its real nature. Because love, however, is the greatest power in the Universe, it follows that if we work against it we hurt ourselves greatly, for the greater the love, the greater the disharmony and suffering for the one who opposes it.

Thus, we see that God does not punish us, but is always love, and that we punish ourselves by putting ourselves outside Love. Actually, so it seems to me, what takes place in the next life is that we have an environment which corresponds to our habitual thought-life. If we have a heavenly mind and thus think heavenly thoughts, then we will find ourselves in a heavenly environment. It is only in this way that we could ever be happy and comfortable. If a man with a hellish mind were put in a heaven of purity, love and perfection, he would be tortured and tormented beyond endurance. That would not be the fault of heaven, but of the man's mind. Therefore, Jesus said: "Change your minds, for the Kingdom of heaven approaches."

The other cause of much suffering is the belief that God sends sickness and disease in order to make us good. But Jesus never taught any such thing. Instead, He healed all who were brought to Him. If sickness and disease are sent by God to make us good, then Jesus worked against God by healing the sick; and also, all doctors and nurses are likewise the enemies of God and of their patients. If it were true that God sends disease and sickness, then it would be only logical for us to try to become as diseased as possible so that we might become good; and also, to put all doctors and nurses into prison so that they could no longer try to prevent our being made good by being diseased and full of sickness.

What I am trying to bring out and emphasise by all this is simply this: that God desires for us only our highest good and wants us all to be blest: that He is showering His blessing upon us at all times. God is the good and perfect one - good absolute and perfection absolute - He is life and light, wisdom and love; wholeness and completeness; joy and peace, and all manner of divine good, and also, He is beyond all our conceptions of Divine Good. The desire of Heaven is that we should be blest and that we should make manifest God's idea concerning each of us, which is perfection. The real truth about each one of us is God's idea about us, held eternally in the mind of God. Unfortunately, deeply buried in our subconscious mind is a contrary idea - the idea that God loves to afflict us with all manner of plagues, and that He delights to play with us, like a cat playing with a mouse. Because of this erroneous belief (Jesus called it being bound by Satan), we manifest all manner of disease and sickness, and then insult God by attributing it all to Him.

If we can but become freed from this enslaving idea what a difference it will make to the world! What a difference it would make if all people, or if all who believe in God, were to believe that He is a God of good and not evil, or even a mixture of good and evil! Expecting disease, or thinking that it is inevitable, or that God sends it, tends to produce disease. The belief acts as an auto-suggestion.

How, then, can this widespread error be overcome, seeing that we have nearly all our spiritual leaders against us, who still continue to teach their followers that God cannot deliver them from trouble and that He sends disease in order to make them good? Well, it certainly does seem hopeless, when we think of all the thousands of preachers and teachers who are so busily engaged in destroying such little faith as their followers, in spite of the spirit of the times, may still possess. But it does not rest with us. God is omnipotent and brings everything to pass, at the right time. All that we can do, at present at any rate, is to put our own house in order: to cleanse our own mind of erroneous ideas. We can impress this thought on our subconscious mind. "God is good, and He fills my life with good". Or "God omnipotent is the one source, and He is Good. Therefore, nothing but good can come to me."

Chapter Twenty-Two

Our Highest Good

But seek ye first the Kingdom of God and His righteousness, and all these things shall be added unto you.
Matthew 6:33

God is not a God of penury and lack, any more than He is a God of disease and sickness. He does not send disease and sickness, neither does He condemn us to a life of penury and lack. God desires for us only our highest good - a state of well-being that is far better than we could either think or imagine. God's ways are perfect, and He desires for us only that which is perfect, otherwise He would not be perfect.

The teaching of Jesus on this subject is most illuminating, but like the rest of the Sermon on the Mount, it is seldom taught and even less seldom put into practise.

The first thing that He taught was that we should give up struggling and striving for wealth and possessions: that we should not "lay up treasure on earth where moth and rust doth corrupt and where thieves break through and steal": that we should not be anxious about tomorrow, nor even to worry about our food and clothing; but that we could trust our Heavenly Father to supply us with everything necessary at the right time, without fail. In other words, that we should not work for gain, but as an act of loving service. If we serve life in this way, then whatever we may need in the way of supply will come to us just at the right time.

Actually, if we could but realise it, we are provided for from the cradle to the grave. Jesus pointed this out when He likened our position to that of the fowls of the air and the flowers of the field.

"Behold the fowls of the air: for they sow not, neither do they reap, nor gather into barns: yet your Heavenly Father feeds them. ... Are ye not much better than they? And why take ye (anxious) thought for raiment? Consider the lilies of the field how they grow, they toil not, neither do they spin: and yet I say unto you that even Solomon in all his glory was not arrayed like one of these".

From this it will be seen that Jesus did not teach poverty, or penury and lack. Indeed, He shows clearly that it is the divine intention that all our needs should be supplied in no skimping way. Some people's idea is that Jesus and His disciples went about in rags and tatters, begging for crusts. There is, of course, nothing in the Gospels to support such a view. There is no evidence that they were not adequately clothed. As we read, we do not find a single hint of a shortage of anything. They always had money with which to buy whatever they needed. Also, there was sufficient money in the bag to give to the poor. They never regarded themselves as poor, but they spoke of the poor as a class apart, a class to be pitied and helped. But they never looked to be helped themselves. Everything that they needed must have come to them at the right time.

When Jesus sent out His disciples, He sent them without purse or scrip and without change of raiment, so that they had no material means at all. They were not to beg but were to go where the Spirit led them. After they had returned, Jesus said to them: "Lacked ye anything?" And they answered, "No".

The popular idea that Jesus and his disciples were a poverty-stricken band of ragged beggars is therefore quite erroneous. What Jesus taught was that we should not depend upon possessions, upon usury, upon exploiting our fellow man, or upon any worldly method which would force people less fortunate than ourselves to contribute to our comfort or even luxury, through unjust economic necessity. What He taught was that we should serve life and our fellows in love and freedom, without expecting or demanding a reward, and that if we would do this, then life would see to it that we should lack nothing.

In these days it is not always possible to avoid possessions altogether, for the workman owns his tools, and in order to enjoy security of tenure he may own the house in which he lives, and also there is his bicycle, etc. Then the businessman may employ a certain amount of capital, and so on. But if he regards all these things as not his personal possessions, but simply for him to use for the general good, he will be alright. He will be alright because he will be living according to the spirit of the teaching of Jesus.

With regard to saving for old age and life insurance against old age, this is a vexed subject, over which there is much difference of opinion. Each one must do as he or she feels led to do. The course of action which gives him inward peace will be the right one for each individual. There is much to be said both for and against. If we do insure, however, and save reasonably, we must be careful not to lean on these things but must rely upon God. These things may fail, but God can never fail.

The thing to avoid is dependence upon money. If we depend upon money, it may take to itself wings and leave us, just like sand running through our fingers. Whereas, if we depend upon God, then we find that we are supported in the day of adversity.

We have to remember that God is the spiritual cause of all substance. "The silver is mine, and the gold is mine, says the Lord", and "the cattle on a thousand hills". If we rely upon God, then we rely on the Cause of all manifest substance, and therefore we are supported, when others who put their trust in riches may find themselves stranded.

But, in addition, we must not cling to money or hoard it if we are to enjoy the freedom of which Jesus speaks. Money should be kept in circulation if it is to do its duty. If we keep a £1 note in our pocket, while at the same time we owe £1 to a tradesman, we do the community a disservice, because we cause a congestion or block in the circulation. Money is the lifeblood of our social and business life, and, like the circulation of the blood in the body, must not be impeded. If we have a clot in our blood, so that the circulation is impeded, serious bodily trouble will be the result. It is the same with the circulation of money: if we impede it serious results follow. If we keep money in our pocket which ought to be paid to the tradesman, then he cannot pay his wholesaler, and the wholesaler cannot pay the manufacturer, and the manufacturer cannot pay his rent or his employees. If, however, we pay the money to the tradesman, he can pay his wholesaler, his wholesaler can pay his manufacturer, and the manufacturer can pay his rent or his employees, so that everyone concerned is benefited through the healthy circulation which is set in motion.

If we keep money circulating, it not only benefits others, but it also keeps us in a state of good financial health. Also, the knowledge that everything is paid for and that we own nothing, frees us from care and makes us feel financially free and light-hearted.

There is such a thing as a divine prosperity, a prosperity which is of God, and which is due to God's blessing resting upon us. We find this well set out in Psalm 1 and in Jeremiah 17: 5-8. One who lives righteously and who trusts in the Lord and makes Him his hope and who meditates on the Law of God, is likened to a tree which is planted by a river, so that its roots are always moist in spite of dry seasons. Such a tree flourishes during times of drought, when other trees are withered. Of such a man Psalm 1 says that "whatsoever he does shall prosper".

Of course, to live in this way is to live a life of faith. We have to learn to give and to give freely. If we cling to money, we tend to impoverish ourselves, but if we give, we become freed and blessed.

This is summed up in the words of scripture, Proverbs 11:24: "There is one who scatters, yet increases more; and there is one who withholds more than is right, but it leads to poverty."

This brings us to the subject of tithing, about which I'm often asked to write. I have always been reluctant to respond to this request, having read so much that had been written on this subject, which I did not like. Readers were told that tithing was the way to prosperity, and that if they wanted to be prosperous all that they had to do was to tithe a tenth of their income, like the children of Israel used to do, and they would flourish amazingly.

This was in very bad taste, to say the least of it, and also not quite true. It was just enough 'off truth' to prove misleading. Also, through misleading people it was liable to attract the wrong type of person. For, if one were to persuade people to start tithing in order to make money out of it, then no divine blessing could rest on the effort, and without the divine blessing, we cannot be truly successful or prosperous in anything. The people who would be attracted by such promises would not be of the type who would endure the tests of discipleship. When trials of their faith came, they would soon be discouraged and "go back to the beggarly elements of the world". Also, they would not succeed, because what they did was from a wrong motive. If we do what on the surface may appear to be good, from a wrong motive, then we cannot succeed. The motive is the all-important thing.

I think it is wrong to entice people to tithe by promising them that they will become prosperous by so doing; because if they were to tithe from such a motive, I do not think that they would become prosperous. There is no objection, however, to the teaching of the practise of tithing done from the right motive, tithing should be done for its own sake, and not in order to reap a reward. It merely means giving to the Lord's work on a systematic basis. It liberates us from that poverty complex described in the book of proverbs, which I have already quoted: "There is that (which) withholds more than is met, but it tends to poverty". If we tithe with the idea of reaping a rich reward, we do not become freed from the poverty complex which may have a stranglehold on us, consequently it cannot set us free. Also, if we tithe with the idea of reward we make our gifts with reluctance, so that we are still attached to money - we do not become free.

It is after giving from a pure motive, thinking of and looking for no reward, that we enter into freedom. It is then that it becomes possible for God to bless us. It is then that the invisible account of our life becomes balanced, and when that takes place a state of blessedness becomes possible.

It has been said that there is an invisible profit and loss account kept of our life. With most of us, I am afraid, it is very much on the wrong side. At any rate, it is so in my case. We have received so much and have given so little. All our life we have been receiving so much blessing from our Heavenly Father, and in return, alas, we have given so little. Every possible form of Divine good has been heaped upon us; yet we have taken it all for granted, and perhaps have never yet really said "thank you". We have received so much from Heaven yet how little have we given back in thankfulness, thanksgiving, gratitude, love, service and substance to God and humanity!

All the blessings of this life we owe to Heaven and our Father in Heaven. All that we have at the present time, and all that we are receiving week by week come from the Lord. If we feel grateful for it all, and thank God for it, and bless the channel through which it comes, it makes us want to give something back in return, by supporting the Lord's work in some form or other.

By tithing, or by giving freely to the Lord's work, we become freed from the tyranny of money. We become freer financially, although our means may not increase. Some people start with one tenth of their income and increase it as the years go by. Some find that their income increases; others that what they have seems to go farther; while in most cases there is a sense of blessedness and security which comes through trusting money less and God more.

To part with our money in this way is an act of faith. We cannot see how we are going to get on without it, so we have to throw ourselves upon God, and rely upon Him to see us through.

We may experience bad times of doubt and fear, when we wonder apprehensively what will happen and what the end of it will be. This throws us more completely upon God than ever, so that all we can do is to take hold of His hand, metaphorically speaking, and go forward, stepping out into the unknown with Him. Then we find that we are brought through our difficulty, and we find a sense of liberty and freedom on the other side of it, and also a feeling of greater security in God.

No, God does not want us to be poverty-stricken, but that we should have every need met. What He wants is that we should be free from the power of Mammon, relying upon the Lord, instead of being enslaved by money and modern economic conditions. He wants us to give and to work, not for reward, but as an act of love and service to God and our fellow man.

Worldly people will still work and struggle according to worldly standards and their lives will continue to be full of strain and anxious striving. But God wants His children to live according to Heavenly standards, working in a spirit of love and service instead of for reward, and giving in the same spirit, looking to Him to see them through. God wants us to live lives of harmony and freedom from all anxiety and care; to be entirely free from every burden and every fear.

When I was comparatively young, I found how easy it is to make money to come our way. It is an attitude of mind, really, instead of mentally running after money, we mentally see and realise that money is running after us. But if we accumulate such money, hoard it, or put it out at interest, it brings to us all manner of trouble and disaster. At any rate, that has been my experience. But I have also found that if we acknowledge that it is not ours, but that it only comes through our hands in order for us to circulate it in the form of good works, we remain free. Indeed, we enjoy a wonderful freedom in financial matters, so that it is like being a millionaire, without suffering from the many disadvantages and burdens which great riches bring. Many people feel that they would like to be rich because they would then be financially free. They would have no debts and they would not have to think: "can I afford this, or can I afford that?" That is the only advantage of being rich, whereas the disadvantages are many and grievous.

When, however, we have gained the financial freedom which comes through non-attachment to Mammon and a looking instead to spiritual sources, we find that all our needs are met perfectly, just at the right moment, so that we do not have to be anxious for the morrow, but can live just as Jesus taught - without a care in the world.

Chapter Twenty-Three

Divine Good

Greater is he that is in you than he that is in the world.
1 John, 4:4 (KJV)

In previous chapters we have seen that it is the divine intention that we should be neither diseased nor poverty-stricken, but that our life should be blest and that we should enjoy all manner of divine good.

It does not follow that because God wants us to enjoy the highest good and desires that we should be Divinely blest that we shall not have to meet with trials of our faith and difficult experiences. Actually, it is only in this way that we can become men and women of faith and attain to the carefree life which Jesus promises. It is through meeting such experiences that we are initiated into the mysteries of the life lived in God and learn to know God so well that we can trust Him at all times and in all circumstances. If we meet all experiences in the right way, then for us they are all good, although some may appear to be evil.

In this life we cannot have sunshine all the way, because in the nature of things there must be light and shade and experiences which we call good and those which we may call evil.

It is how we meet these things which matters. For instance, what we call a good experience, when everything goes smoothly and we are greatly prospered, may prove our undoing, if we allow such things to cause us to become spiritually slack and our soul to slumber. On the other hand, a bout of adversity may throw us back upon God, so that we learn to know Him better, and our inner life becomes quickened and strengthened. Thus, what we call good may be turned into evil, and what we call evil into good.

To live as Jesus taught, although so desirable, cannot be achieved by wishful thinking, or daydreaming, or half-hearted effort. The life of freedom and liberation such as Jesus taught, which is a state of complete emancipation from the dark powers of disease on the one hand, and the fear of penury and also the power of Mammon, on the other, is a state of attainment which has to be won through the exercise of faith.

Nothing that is really worth having can be had without working for it. The more precious the object we seek, the more closely it is guarded. This is as it should be, and it explains why Jesus said that we should not cast our pearls before swine. He meant, of course, that we should not attempt to pass the secrets of advanced Divine Truth onto people who are not yet ready for such knowledge. We may do great harm by making such attempts. Also, it explains those mysterious statements that some are prevented from understanding Truth, and that their ears are holden that they should not hear, etc. This merely means that such people are kept from understanding because they're not anything like ready. Truth, if revealed to those who are not ready, would be very hurtful; so, for his own sake the man who is not yet ready must be, as it were, protected from Truth.

> Eternal Light, Eternal Light,
> How pure the soul must be,
> When placed within Thy searching sight,
> It shrinks not, but with calm delight,
> May live and look on Thee.

Again, those who are unready must be prevented from seizing arcane powers and using them to their own imagined self-interest and to the detriment of others. It would be like allowing a child to be put in charge of an electric power station.

Consequently, the state of attainment which Jesus described and taught is not for the crowd, but for the true disciple - the one who is willing to leave all and follow Him.

In order to reach the state of attainment in which we can enjoy "the glorious liberty of the children of God", we have to live a life of faith, so that, like Paul, we can say, "The life I now live in the flesh, I live by the faith of the Son of God".

This is the secret of all achievement in the life of faith - to realise that we are one with the Son of God, or in a state of union with Christ in us. Norman Grubb, in his book *Touching the Invisible* (Lutterworth Press), says:

> All believers say in a general way, "God is almighty", or "God can do this or that". Only one in a thousand says "God is almighty in *me*", and "God will do so and so through *me.*"

Within *you* is the Power. "Greater is he that is in you than he that is in the world". Armed with this knowledge we can face successfully all life's experiences; overcome every trial and seeming evil; rise victorious over every difficulty; and pass triumphantly through each initiation.

It is not meant that we should lead easy lives, but we are called to live lives which are victorious over difficulty. One who chose an easy life would also be a soft and flabby character. He would be like soft iron, which has no quality of hardness, and therefore can never be made into a tempered blade. But one who lives a life full of experience and testing becomes strong, tempered like a keen blade.

As I have already said, the secret of overcoming is to maintain the attitude that we are one with the creative power and intelligence which creates, rules and guides all things and happenings.

So long as we live in a state of separateness, we remain weak and impotent. It is when we realise our oneness with the great creative power that we are able to overcome in every difficult circumstance in which we may find ourselves. We may be faced by what might appear to be complete failure and ruin, either of soul, body or affairs, yet, if we maintain the attitude of oneness with the one infinite power, nothing can prevail against us, any more than it could prevail against God.

"Christ lives in me," said Paul the Apostle. He (Paul) did not do anything, really, it was Christ living in him who did everything. Or, to put it in different words: it was not the outward man of the senses who did the works, but the Christ in him - with whom he was one - who enabled him to overcome impossible tasks.

It was because Paul realised this truth so clearly and because he lived in the faith of the Son of God that he was able to rise above every difficulty.

Jesus taught that we should ask *in His Name*, just the same as He Himself would do, and then whatever we asked would be granted. Not to beg and pray to a God afar off – God up there, and we down here – but in the name of Jesus, with the same authority as though He Himself were speaking. He taught that if we had faith, we could command things to come to pass and they would obey the command and duly take place.

When attempting to live the life of faith we are more likely than not to be tempted over the very thing that we're trying to manifest.

If we want to manifest health, then it may be that we may become worse instead of better. This will try our faith, and if we are shallow rooted, we will probably give up in despair. Or, if we try to live a life of faith as regards supply, trying to put the teaching of Jesus into practise, as given us in Matthew 6, verses 24-34, we may find our finances very difficult to manage. If we are in earnest, however, this will not make us turn back, but rather we shall become all the more determined to win through to liberty and freedom.

As already stated, the great secret is for each one of us to take up the attitude that, "He that is in me is greater than he that is in the world," and that the indwelling spirit and my true self are one. Our troubles and difficulties may appear to be insuperable, but if we take our stand in the Infinite in this way, they simply cannot prevail over us.

In order to attain to the carefree state, we have to pass through qualifying or initiating experiences. If we are going to win through to that state of real knowledge in which we know and are absolutely certain that it is God who supplies our every need, and that we can depend upon Him completely; just as though we possessed an unlimited bank draft, and even more so, because the bank might fail, but God, never; then we must pass a crucial experience which is so severe, that when it has been passed will give us a sense of absolute certainty. It is obvious that such actual 'knowing' – not belief, or even faith – can be reached only through experience. Such a state of knowing and absolute certainty is faith come to fruition.

Consequently, one who has decided to live by faith may have to pass through what he may think to be a severe apprenticeship. He may even be reduced to his last coin. If so, what is he to do? Is he to draw in his horns and close his purse, and become careful? Not if he is to win through. What he must do is to go forward, for we must always go forward, and act as though all the resources of Heaven were behind us, as indeed they are, although outward circumstances may contradict such an idea. What he must do is give away his coin. He is being subjected to his supreme test, which is really his greatest opportunity, and his whole future depends upon how to act. If he goes back and plays for safety, he is lost and finished. If he goes forward, daring everything, he will win through to liberty and freedom.

But if he should not possess even a shilling, what shall he do? He should give what he has, some article, perhaps, which he values and clings to; or failing that, he should do some helpful work, an act of loving service. Or if that is impossible, let him pray earnestly for someone. In some way we must keep on giving. If we do this then heaven cannot fail to supply us abundantly. It is the law of life.

In our giving we create a vacuum, and this vacuum God fills abundantly according to our faith.

I know a man who gives away the very shoes on his feet; yet he declares that he has never gone unshod in consequence. He says that as good a pair or better has always come almost immediately.

We have to get rid of the mental habit of clinging to things. Instead, we should cultivate a giving attitude. It is in this way that we become freed from a dreadful bondage and servitude. We do indeed become "transformed through the renewing of our mind", and "prove what is that good, and acceptable, and perfect, will of God".

This teaching that we are one with the indwelling spirit may seem advanced to some readers. It is. It is what Paul described as "strong meat", and not "milk for babes". Milk is necessary for babes, while meat would be most unsuitable; but when the child grows up it will have to have more solid food than milk. In the same way, we all outgrow the "milk for babes" stage, and then require the stronger food which the Spirit of Truth has prepared for us.

There is a text which puts the truth of what I have been trying to explain in very concise words. It is: "He that is joined to the Lord is one spirit" (I Corinthians, 6:17). We see, therefore, that we can become joined to the Lord, and that then we become One Spirit, through union. Thus, we can say, when confronted by insuperable difficulties and apparent lack, that He that is in us is greater than he that is in the world, and that we are joined to the Lord within us, and therefore we are One Spirit.

Realising this great truth, we can do as Jesus did - rebuke the winds and the waves of the storms of life, so that there is a great calm.

We can say: "The Lord in me is health and wholeness. Interiorly, I am joined to the Lord, and we are one spirit, expressing and manifesting God's perfect idea."

Or, when faced with the chill blast of the winds of adversity we can declare: "The spirit of the Lord in me is the spirit of infinite and abundant supply of every need. We are one spirit, expressing and manifesting the substance of God."

Such wording is merely suggestive. Each one can think of something similar but couched in his own language. The idea is to affirm and realise that God is mighty in us, and that through us He is manifesting all manner of good and raising us to higher and better things. We have to unite ourselves with the Almighty Spirit within us, so that we become one, and then go forward, knowing that together, as one Spirit, we can never fail.

This mental attitude on our part may produce a violent reaction from the world. But, if we stand steadfast in the truth, the worst that men and circumstances can do to us cannot hurt us but can only provide us with the material for further advancement, thus raising us to higher and better things. The greater the opposition we meet, the more progress we make, and the more truly successful we become.

As this little book has endeavoured to show: God does not want us to be sick, diseased, or poverty stricken, but rather to be richly and abundantly blest. The teaching of Jesus was that it is possible to reach a life of freedom from care and anxiety with every need, both

GOD THE SOURCE OF GOOD

spiritual and material, adequately supplied. This state, described as "the glorious liberty of the children of God", can be attained to through living a life of faith, trusting the Lord (the one source of life and eternal substance) and through affirming and realising our oneness with Him. "Greater is He that is in you, than he that is in the world.

> He that is joined to the Lord is One Spirit.

If you have enjoyed reading this book, please consider taking just a moment to leave a review on Amazon. Reviews help to boost the visibility of a book so that others may find it and benefit from reading it. Thank you very much – your effort is much appreciated.

If you are in the US, use this code

Scan the QR code or type this link into your browser

bit.ly/3G3ujUN

Scan with your phone camera

Hamblin Vision Publishing

THANK YOU!

If you are in the UK, use this code

Scan the QR code or type this link into your browser

bit.ly/4exwyfI

Scan with your phone camera

Hamblin Vision Publishing

THANK YOU!

If you are in the Canada, use this code

Scan the QR code or type this link into your browser

bit.ly/3I4Qavy

Scan with your phone camera

Hamblin Vision Publishing

THANK YOU!

If you are in the Australia, use this code

Scan the QR code or type this link into your browser

bit.ly/3ZY9bWC

Scan with your phone camera

Hamblin Vision Publishing

THANK YOU!

Also by Henry Thomas Hamblin

Other books by Henry Thomas Hamblin

The Stillness of the Infinite: 18 Meditations to Deepen Spiritual Awareness through the Progressive Reflective Meditation Method

The Power of Thought: How to unlock the power of your mind to create a life of health, success, and prosperity

Within You is the Power: The Inner Secrets to Health, Happiness, Success and Abundance

The Secrets of Your Divine Powers: Reconnect with your Spiritual Self to Overcome Obstacles, Heal your Life and Achieve True Success

The Spiritual Path to True Success: The Practical Mystic's Guide to Living Successfully

The Message of a Flower: The Divine Wisdom in Nature

The Worry Antidote: The Practical Mystic's Guide to Living Fearlessly

To purchase the following titles please visit our website:
www.thehamblinvision.org.uk

    The Way of the Practical Mystic

    My Search for Truth

    The Story of my Life

    Life Without Strain

    Divine Adjustment

    The Open Door

    Life of the Spirit

His Wisdom Guiding

The Hamblin Book of Daily Readings

God Our Centre and Source

God's Sustaining Grace

www.ingramcontent.com/pod-product-compliance
Lightning Source LLC
Chambersburg PA
CBHW030336010526
44119CB00047B/514